ON CENSORSHIP

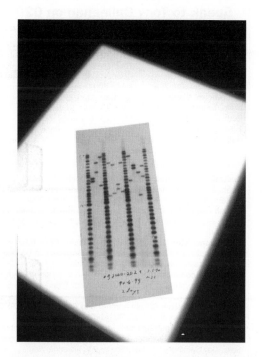

INDEX ON CENSORSHIP 3 2000

INDEX

Volume 29 No 3 May/June 2000 Issue 194

WEBSITE NEWS UPDATED WEEKLY

www.indexoncensorship.org
contact@indexoncensorship.org
tel: 020 7278 2313
fax: 020 7278 1878

Index on Censorship (ISSN 0306-4220) is published bi-monthly by a non-profit-making company: Writers & Scholars International Ltd, Lancaster House, 33 Islington High Street, London N1 9LH. *Index on Censorship* is associated with Writers & Scholars Educational Trust, registered charity number 325003
Periodicals postage: (US subscribers only) paid at Newark, New Jersey. Postmaster: send US address changes to *Index on Censorship* c/o Mercury Airfreight International Ltd Inc, 365 Blair Road, Avenel, NJ 07001, USA

Subscriptions (6 issues per annum)
Individuals: UK £39, US $52, rest of world £45
Institutions: UK £44, US $80, rest of world £50
Speak to Tony Callaghan on 020 7278 2313

EDITORIAL

Privacy on parade

'Big Brother is finally here,' said a British MP on hearing last month that MI5 is planning to monitor all emails and Internet messages. He underestimates the problem. Hundreds of global little brothers are already watching and intervening in our lives. Mass surveillance is everywhere, set up not not just for the benefit of governments and espionage services but as much for powerful corporations and the free market. Surveillance cameras (p45), credit-reporting agencies, data matching and the information gathering of e-commerce have put us in a goldfish bowl in which our activities, habits and tastes are observed and recorded. Even our DNA, Simon Davies tells us, may soon be on databases (p36). *Index* looks at these threats to our privacy and their intimate links with the Internet – for, as Bruce Sterling says in his ominously predictive article, 'technology marches while the law crawls'(p74).

John Naughton warns that with e-commerce, cyberspace, 'the most gloriously open, unregulated public space in human history', could easily become the most controlled environment imaginable – with no attempts to balance the needs of society against commercial imperatives (p116). David Banisar tells us how dotcom companies are gathering 'financial records, medical records, reading habits, political opinions, sexual interests', which may be sold on to advertisers or used by government or individuals in any number of ways (p53). Yaman Akdeniz fears that the crucial right to anonymity and cryptography online in reporting human rights abuses and whistle-blowing will be undermined by law enforcement agencies (p57).

Privacy is not just about hiding things: it is about autonomy and self-possession, an aspect of our civil rights. And though millions of people in the developing world are not yet touched by these issues, it probably won't be long before they are. India, as Salil Tripathi tells us, is experiencing an infotech revolution (p146) while John Gittings reports an exponential growth of the Web in China (p123). In an age of the 'global flight of data', how do we safeguard the person while defending freedom of speech? *Index*'s contributors suggest some startling answers.

Meanwhile, in the old world of print, free expression remains as threatened as ever. In Iran, just after Easter, a flurry of newspapers and journals – 16 in all – were banned and two newspaper editors summoned before a Revolutionary Court, in continued conservative attempts to undo the gains of Iran's reformers. Another reminder for us at *Index*, as if we needed it, of why we exist. ❑

contents

Is privacy censorship? With free expression and privacy both human rights, how can a balance be struck?

p34

The Internet was a dream for globalists, promising equality and communication for the developing world. The boom in e-commerce may have killed off those ideals

p114

Poland's war on porn has awakened old prejudices and new fears p17

LETTERS

The curtain falls
From Sandy Smith Madsen, Atlanta

Elizabeth Wilson's article (Index 2/00) is interesting. There is, however, an embarrassing error in paragraph five. The Seneca Falls Women's Rights Convention of 1848 is widely acknowledged as the official onset of the organised women's movement in the US. This event was conceived, organised and convened by Elizabeth Cady Stanton, Lucretia Mott and like-minded cohorts. The idea that the women forced themselves to sit behind a curtain is, of course, ludicrous.

The author has this historic event confused with the World Anti-Slavery Convention of London (1840), at which Stanton and Mott were indeed excluded from participation and forced by the men to sit behind a curtain. The seriousness of this error is in the realm of placing Dred Scott as a Founding Father in attendance at the Constitutional Convention.

Response to Njabulo Ndebele
From David Beresford, Cape Town

I'm not sure whether to be amused, or alarmed by your publication of the article by Professor Njabulo Ndebele, denouncing the *Mail & Guardian* for alleged racism. A footnote to the article states that Ndebele 'submitted a version of this article to the *Mail & Guardian* which declined to publish it'.

I am a former correspondent of the *Guardian* in South Africa. I was peripherally involved in the purchase of the *Mail & Guardian* (then the *Weekly Mail*) by the *Guardian*. Since then a health problem has forced me into semi-retirement, but the editor, Phillip van Niekerk, flatters me by seeking advice from me from time to time.

He did so when he received a 1,000-word letter for publication from Ndebele, commenting on a strident exchange between the *M&G* and the office of the South African President. The editor's problem was fundamentally one of space. Ndebele did not want the letter cut and the letter itself misrepresented the *M&G* in a number of respects.

Ndebele had no *locus standi* with regard to the original dispute, other than the wish to air his views. A great deal of space had already been expended on the debate. An article of more than 1,000 words was exceptional in such a small publication, much less a letter to the editor. On top of that the *M&G* would be required to refute each misrepresentation, which would have demanded even more space. But if he declined to publish it, predicted van Niekerk, 'we'll be accused of being racists'.

It was one of those occasions when one is only too happy to dish out advice, so seemingly clear-cut were the issues at stake. My advice was that he make a brief policy statement on the letters page, explaining space constraints and even suggesting, for guidance in this age of electronic word-counts, a length of say 400–500 words, in excess of which a letter would rarely be published.

At the same time, I suggested to him, announce that the 'right' still enjoyed by reporters as well as the editor to append replies to letters critical of them and the newspaper was being abolished. As a corollary, I advised him, tell readers that no misrepresentations of fact would be allowed in letters and point out that disputes as to the basis of such 'fact' could be taken to the press ombudsman, or litigation. As for Ndebele, I said, explain the space problems and ask him to cut his letter to 400–500 words and publish it without comment or reply. 'But he'll say I've rejected his article, because I'm a racist,' persisted van Niekerk. 'No he won't,' I scoffed in effect. 'Ndebele is a reasonable man.'

So far as I am aware all of my advice was followed. The letter, at reasonable length, was never published, because Ndebele failed to take up the invitation. Van Niekerk last week phoned to announce that, not only had Ndebele never replied to the invitation, but the 'letter' transmogrified into an 'article' which the M&G had 'declined to publish' had been published in *Index on Censorship* 2/00 charging van Niekerk with 'racism'. With an eye to the length of this letter I will not bother to deal with the rubbish which Ndebele's letter/article contains. Instead I would commend to your readership a reading of van Niekerk's statement to the Human Rights Commission (*www.mg.co.za*) which is not only an incisive repudiation of the sort of rubbish peddled by such as Ndebele, but which contains some of the most admirable statements I have heard in support of non-racialism and freedom of expression in the South African context.

Further response
From Phillip van Niekerk, editor, Mail & Guardian

Njabulo Ndebele abuses his considerable reputation when he does not make clear to *Index* readers that he and the *Mail & Guardian* have been at loggerheads for a few years now (*Index* 2/2000). While vice-chancellor of the University of the North at Turfloop in South Africa, Ndebele faced considerable difficulties in the late 1990s from the university's arcane politics – difficulties on which we reported.

But the main cause of bad blood between Ndebele and the *M&G* arose from a series of articles we published on the affairs of a private education company, Edupark. The gist was that Ndebele had presided over the illicit transfer of R20m (US$2.98m) to Edupark. Much of *M&G*'s reportage was based on the findings of an inquiry chaired by a solicitor, Phineas Mojapelo.

Since, in his article for *Index*, Ndebele accuses us of racism and of seeking to undermine black notables, we should specify that our reporter on the story, the solicitor who headed the inquiry and the university council chairman who condemned Ndebele are all black.

Since that exchange, Ndebele has seemed intent on attributing malign motive to the *M&G*. We have had to ask ourselves why. The best answer we have managed to come up with is that he has concluded that the best way to rubbish the unfortunate funding row is to rubbish the newspaper

which most fully covered it, ours – a newspaper which, notwithstanding Ndebele's best efforts to undermine our standing, has an enviable reputation for independence and for favouring no one, whether they be black, white, left, right or indifferent, whether working under apartheid or in our new democracy.

[*Index* writes: Professor Njabulo Ndebele, an award-winning author with at least ten years experience in university management, was never charged in connection with the inquiry's findings:

'The chair of the university council, Benny Boshielo, was suspended for mismanagement and later apologised to Ndebele for accusing him of being party to the scandal.' *Mail & Guardian* 14 April 2000.

In April, Professor Ndebele was appointed vice-chancellor of the University of Cape Town with the unanimous approval of the university council.]

Correction

The reference to Elena Lappin's article ' The Man with Two Heads' (*Granta #66*) on the Wilkormirski hoax, was inadvertently left out of Norman Finkelstein's article in our last issue. Apologies to both authors.❏

● **False note** Three Cambodian songs were banned in March for 'debasing the country's women'. Minister of women's affairs Mu Sochua said 'the songs portray women like toys, instead of human beings' and highlighted only the negative side of Cambodian society. The writer of one of them, Fay Sam Ang, said they merely conveyed the realities of life.

● **Flight of the song thrush** Relations between Ankara and Ashgabat cooled after a Turkish singer accompanying a Turkish delegation to the Turkmenistan capital rejected the amorous clutches of President Saparmurat Niyazov, reported the *Süddeutsche Zeitung* in February. The paper said Turkish authorities have 'leaned on' the woman not to divulge details of the episode to the Turkish press.

● **Emperor's new Quran** President-for-Life Saparmurat Niyazov of Turkmenistan has ordered the burning of all copies of a translation of the Quran, briefly jailing its state-appointed translator, before commuting his sentence to internal exile for life. 'Khoja Ahmed Orazgylych, together with the writer Atamyrat Atabayev … translated it from Uzbek to Turkmen and, as a result, it lost any meaning. I have ordered that all [copies of] the new translation be collected and burned. This translation is evil.' Niyazov clearly was not just upset by linguistics: '[Orazgylych] has long been ... committed to evil deeds. He has been visited by childless women, given them talismans, courted them and sometimes committed offences.' A possible cause for Niyazov's displeasure was an interview Orazgylych gave to Radio Liberty criticising Niyazov's incorporation of a Christmas tree into his self-aggrandising New Year celebrations.

● **Segregated dating** Bob Jones University in Greenville, South Carolina, has slightly relaxed a regulation dating from the 1950s that bans interracial relationships. Students at the Baptist university can now go out in mixed-race couples on condition that they have written consent from their parents. Bob Jones III, president of the university and grandson of its founder, explained that 'when you date or marry interracially, it cuts you off from people'.

● **Letter of the law** In March, Turkish authorities opened investigations into six local newspapers for their use of the letter 'W' in articles on Kurdish spring celebrations. Kemal Celik, editor of the south-eastern newspaper *Batman Postasi*, reported that the paper was being investigated for spelling the name of the 21 March festival, *Newroz*, with a 'W' rather than a 'V', as in the Turkish equivalent, *Nevruz*. The Kurdish New Year celebration has only recently been recognised by Turkey.

● **Good news in Kurdish** The Supreme Court in Turkey decided in March that citizens could finally give their children Kurdish names. Last year, Nezir Durak filed a petition asking for his daughter's name to be amended on her identity card from Hatice to Mizgin, because Mizgin is what she is called at home. Previously, all children had to be given Turkish names. Mizgin means 'good news' in Kurdish.

● **Namely, Genghis** Meanwhile, Mongolia's plan to introduce its people to surnames before 15 March has backfired: as many as one million have chosen the name 'Borjigon' to emphasise the belief that they are all descended from Genghis Khan. Until the early part of the twentieth century, Mongolians used clan names with their given names, but these were jettisoned as 'feudal remnants' when Mongolia became the world's second communist state in 1921.

● **Bang ban** Four pupils, aged four and five, were briefly suspended from nursery school in Sayreville, New Jersey, for using their fingers as guns in a game of cops and robbers. The children were heard shouting 'I shot you' and 'Boom, I have a bazooka' during break. School principal Georgia Baumann explained that in these sensitive times, 'It may be just a game ... but it can be taken differently by other children.'

● **Licenced to speak** Singapore plans to establish its own 'Speaker's Corner', based on the London institution, where individuals will be free to speak their mind on mattters that exercise them. But home affairs minister Wong Kan Seng rather spoiled it all when he added that speakers would still need a permit and must respect the tough local libel laws. Last year, an opposition politician, Chee Soon Juan (*Index* 2/1999), was arrested for making a speech on the street in the business district.

● **Excised** A package containing documents advising Iraqis on human rights and press freedom was blocked by Whitehall as a result of UN sanctions, it was reported on 18 February. The package, sent by the free expression watchdog Article 19 to Mosul University in northern Iraq, was returned with an anonymous notice saying that if customers wished to send 'goods' they should first obtain an export licence from the Department of Trade and Industry. Three years ago, the British Library informed an Iraqi member that it could not send him a copy of James Joyce's *Ulysses* due to sanctions, but that he was free to come and use the library – if he could get there.

● **Lewd windows** Marcelle Thomas Bremner, owner of Second Hand Swank, thought she understood the sales potential of her double-fronted clothes shop in the Scottish village of Moniaive. Last November, to the delight of local children, she transformed the window display into a vast homage to the Barbie doll. Business picked up, but the police did not approve. In April, a policewoman visited to say that she thought it disgusting that Ken, Barbie's boyfriend, was sitting next to other male dolls and that Barbie herself was not fully dressed. Marcelle is awaiting a summons for having 'lewd windows'.

● **On the campaign trail** Sales of President Vladimir Putin's book, *In the First Person: Conversations*, were banned in Russia from 13 March until after the presidential election on the grounds that it contained campaign material. The Central Election Commission said any copies reaching the public before the elections must be free. The campaign did precisely that and 50,000 copies were used as handouts. Meanwhile, several *duma* (parliament) deputies lashed out at the 12 March edition of the satirical Spitting Image-style puppet programme *Kukly*. Igor Igoshin, chairman of the agro-industrial group, said many deputies were 'deeply offended by the portrayal of the *duma* as a brothel and our leaders as prostitutes'.

● **Uptight and cold-pressed** Practitioners of the ancient Turkish sport of Yagli Güres, or oil wrestling, are trying to stop a group of homosexuals coming to watch their annual contest at Kirkpinar. The burly wrestlers cover themselves in olive oil and grapple in tight, leather trousers. Protests have arisen because a gay group, the 'Bears of Turkey', are now advertising a tour to the 639th championships later in the year. 'It's immoral, and we are asking for this disgusting business to be stopped,' said Alper Yazoglu, chairman of the Traditional Sports Federation. The wrestlers have to pin each other to the ground to win the contest. Putting a hand down an opponent's trousers to get a better grip is a common tactic.

● **Sins of the fathers** On 7 March, following an initiative by the Irish Labour Party, the Irish Censorship Board has unbanned 420 books, two-thirds of the total on its list of prohibited publications. Many have long since been accepted as standard works; others are reference books, now long out of print.

Most were prohibited because they were seen as 'advocating the unnatural prevention of conception or procurement of abortion or miscarriage'. Even when contraception became legal in 1979, the books remained on the list.

The unbanned list (p97) underlines the bizarre nature of past decisions. It includes literary works such as H.G. Wells' *The Work, Wealth and Happiness of Mankind*, banned in 1932, and Simone de Beauvoir's *A History of Sex* and *Nature of the Second Sex*, banned in 1961 and 1963. Marie Stopes features prominently on the list, with *Birth Control Today* banned in 1936 and again in 1959, and *Change of Life in Men and Women* also outlawed in 1952. Upton Sinclair's *The Book of Love* suffered a similar fate in 1935, as did Bertrand Russell's *Marriage and Morals* in 1930.

The censorship system, which once banned the work of many of Ireland's most celebrated authors, was amended in the mid-1960s. Since then, the blacklist has been cut from around 10,000 to the current figure of 190. A spokeswoman for the Board said the titles of most of those still on the list 'speak for themselves': she cited as examples *The Sins of Cynthia, Sasha Gets Ravaged, The Rope Above, The Bed Below* and *Butch Boys*.

Anthony Garvey

● **A sticky issue** Job opportunities in Turkish publishing are on the up and up. In March, parliament revised the 50-year-old Law on Artistic and Intellectual Works and it is now obligatory for publishers to sticker the back of every book and videocassette with 'banderoles' issued by the ministry of culture.

According to the Turkish Publishers Association – whose members have had to assign full-time employees to the task – publishers must submit paperwork, including the copyright agreement, invoice, shipping list and an order letter to the printing company, all certified by the ministry of finance, to the ministry of culture. If the book is a translation, a translated and notarised copy of the contract, must also be submitted.

While the measure appears designed to prevent pro-Kurdish texts appearing in any of Turkey's 14,000 bookshops, the economic consequences for mainstream publishers are serious. It took seven employees a week to put the banderoles on the 50,000 print run of Orhan Pamuk's latest thriller *Benim Adim Kirmizi* (My Name is Red). Çetin Tüzüner, president of the Turkish Publishers Association, calls the new rule 'a kind of censorship'. 'It allows the control and censorship of publications ... It will also cost us and take a huge amount of time.'

So far, only 15 books have been denied a banderole. However, the prospect of an industry-wide protest against the measure seems improbable: the penalties for those who refuse to sticker are four years with hard labour and a maximum US$60,000 fine.

Michael Griffin

● **Pyrrhic** The spectacle of one media organisation savaging another is never edifying; when the UK's biggest independent TV news organisation hounds a small, feisty news magazine to death by litigation, it bodes ill for all.

At the end of March, ITN won its libel action against *LM*, and was awarded £375,000 (US$600,000) in damages. *LM* was also left with a legal bill of £500,000 (US$800,000) and consequently ceased publication (*Index* 2/2000).

ITN brought the action following an article accusing ITN of deliberately manipulating an image that subsequently became a turning point in the West's intervention in Bosnia.

'The use of the [libel] law by a large news organisation against a magazine with a circulation of 10,000 could have far-reaching implications for independent and investigative journalism,' says *LM* editor Mick Hume. Defending their action after the victory, ITN journalists Penny Marshall and Ian Williams said, 'Freedom of speech is essential to society. But the freedom to print lies masquerading as the truth ... is not.'❏

Judith Vidal-Hall

ANDRZEJ OSEKA

Porn again

The recent campaign in Poland to ban pornography in all its forms cloaks far more intricate anxieties about freedom – and the EU

In early March, the Polish parliament voted in favour of a complete ban on pornography. Its production or distribution would be made punishable by up to five years' imprisonment if 'hard' porn was involved, up to two years if the pornography was 'soft'.

That was the theory. In practice the parliamentary bill scheduled a return to the legal situation of 20 months ago. On 1 September 1998, a new criminal code was introduced to take account of the political turnabout since the fall of communism. Until then the 1969 code had been in force. Communist censorship was very prudish and its severe prohibitions on pornography were implemented consistently. People arriving from the West had their luggage eagerly searched for pornographic magazines and videos.

When communism fell and censorship was abolished, the country was inundated with imported and locally produced erotica, sex shops, dating agencies open 24 hours a day and offering their clients – as one ad put it – 'shameless girls with insatiable appetites'. Newspaper kiosks turned pink with porn. It flew in the face of the law but the legal system was no longer responding. Everything was forbidden, but nothing carried a penalty.

The 1998 code included a chapter on 'Crimes against sexual freedom and morality' by Marian Filar, a specialist in criminal law. The articles relating to pornography made its distribution punishable by five years' imprisonment if children, animals or violence were involved. Supplying pornography to a 'minor below 25' years also carried a penalty of up to two years in prison. Article 202, Clause 1 was particularly significant.

'Whosoever imposes pornographic material on a person who does not wish it shall be subject to a fine, a restraining order or imprisonment.' This proviso presented a buffer to the porn industry as it pushed its way into the public eye. The new rules were therefore intended to protect the freedom of people looking for pornography but also those who wanted to avoid it.

Right-wing circles saw this as a coup for the moral health of the nation. Their representatives in parliament and the senate launched a campaign against pornography, treating it as a test of strength in their war against liberalism. The representatives involved are not particularly numerous, but they are vocal. Catholic Church support of their case seems little more than a formality. At any rate the Episcopate is not leading the campaign. Nor is the government much concerned. The initiative lies with right-wing political parties such as the Christian National Union, the Polish Federation of Movements to Defend Life, All-Polish Youth and far-right Catholic media, such as the hugely popular Radio Maria and the newspaper *Nasz Dziennik* (Our Daily). These are groups over which the religious hierarchy has little control. They spend their time remonstrating with other Catholic circles (including the bishops) over their dangerous 'openness' and manifestly 'weak faith'. National Christianity has a long tradition in Poland and has drawn on the experience of the far right in America and Canada for some years.

In December 1999, following a heated debate in parliament, amendments were introduced to the 1998 criminal code in the form of the new bill. MPs raised the penalty for distribution of hard porn to ten years' imprisonment. To show someone a picture of two people having sex could, according to these proposals, have brought a sentence identical to that imposed for depriving somebody of their eyesight or beating a victim to death.

The Senate then reduced the penalty for the distribution of hard porn to five years in prison. But its most important amendment was the change to Article 202, Clause 1. In the Senate version this read: 'Whosoever distributes pornographic materials, especially magazines, printed matter or pictures, shall be subject to a fine, a restraining order or up to two years' imprisonment.' It implied a total ban on the distribution of materials deemed pornographic. In the public prosecutor's office, MP Antoni Szymanski was already protesting against an ad for 'West' cigarettes that displayed a woman with bared breasts.

There were no plans to punish consumers of pornography, but the criminal code in its new form would have permitted them to be investigated in order to reach the distributors and producers. Any 'pornographic material' became evidence of a crime. The bill was eventually passed with the Senate's amendments by a majority of four. MPs who were opposed to what they considered an ineffective ban and draconian penalties faced a grand rhetorical onslaught from supporters of the bill. MP Zdzislaw Pupa announced: 'This is a war for Poland, a campaign for the moral dimension. Let the prime minister declare himself: is he for pornography or against it?'

It was all redolent of the abortion debate, when opponents of the ruthless punishment of women who had abortions were presented as supporters of killing unborn children. Today, anyone who doubts the good sense of a radical ban on pornography is – in the eyes of the right – declaring himself 'for pornography', for the demoralisation of the nation, the destruction of the family, paedophilia and so on. Doubtless fear of such labels persuaded many MPs and senators with otherwise moderate views to vote 'against pornography'.

The Office of the Senate published a brochure entitled: 'Pornography – a threat to the family and to society'. This was almost exclusively statements from supporters of a total ban. In it, Krystyna Ostrowska, a psychologist from the University of Warsaw, proposes 'a law founded on a notion of the priority of personal dignity over freedom of choice'. She is outraged by Article 202, Clause1 of the 1998 criminal code where 'the legislator took as his guiding principle the notion of free choice, rejecting the primacy of human dignity reflected in the 1969 code'.

Another Senate specialist, lawyer Andrzej Gierech, stated that 'in line with the slogans of the socio-political doctrine of liberalism, the new law negates the value of many traditional systems to a degree unprecedented even in socialist doctrine'. Gierech refers to the 1969 communist code as a model to be imitated. He also eulogises the criminal codes of Tsarist Russia and Prussia, in force when Poland was under partition (1795–1914), because 'they protected the public good: morality and decency, while our new criminal code gives *de facto* licence for sexual freedom'.

In the Senate brochure liberalism, sexual freedom, free choice are combined into a single negative concept opposed by 'higher values' like the public good, human dignity, morality, decency that should be the only basis of law.

The brochure also includes a text by H. Robert Showers borrowed from a US publication and entitled 'Myths and a false understanding of pornography: what you don't know can hurt you'. Plenty of examples here along the lines of: 'In Florida two boys aged nine and seven were passively involved in their parents' use of pornography. In time, imitating the images they had seen, they sexually abused and killed a six-year-old girl.' The thesis that pornography inevitably leads to rape is a constant refrain in this campaign. During the debate over the amendments, demonstrators outside parliament carried banners saying: 'Pornography today – paedophilia tomorrow.' If such a connection did exist, the number of rapes in Poland would have risen several times over given the vast increase in the supply of pornography over the past ten years. In fact, ministry of justice figures show that numbers have remained stable, at around 2,000 a year.

The right-wing media generally accompany attacks on pornography with condemnations of other social phenomena such as drug abuse, homosexuality, atheism, agnosticism, euthanasia, abortion, liberalism, masons, permissiveness, the New Age movement, the Jewish conspiracy, rock music, minority rights and, most tellingly, support for Europe. All this is dubbed the 'civilisation of death'. According to many defenders of morality, one evil gives rise to another: Europe is conspiring to demoralise and then enslave us.

In February, Mariusz Wegrzyn wrote in *Nasz Dziennik* that Poland is 'a state in which minorities, including sexual minorities, are preferred and promoted' while the majority is humiliated and marginalised. 'Those who remind us about the Polish spirit have been called anti-semites. We have a state in which pornography thrives, but the birth rate is low; a state in which abortion is high...' The author appeals for a just war for the public good so that 'a Catholic Polish nation state' can be created. He concludes: 'Onward, gentlemen! Attack! Hold tight the reins! Or it will be slavery, infamy, disgrace...'

Radio Maria devoted many hours of airtime to fighting pornography, including the comment in one programme that pornography is nefarious not because it induces people to commit crimes but because it is sinful and a crime in itself. Nakedness is evil. Presenters and callers warmed to the subject: 'We must defend ourselves!' A teacher boasted that she had threatened to smash a shop window if the porn didn't go – and sure enough it vanished. Listeners called this 'the religious dimension' since 'a Catholic is responsible for the sin of his brethren'. They also called it democracy, because democracy is about enacting the will of the majority and Poland is nominally 95% Catholic. Somebody spoke about some pornographic photos he had seen. The women wore crosses around their necks. 'Not Stars of David,' he said, emphatic and triumphant. 'You can see right away who it is they want to disgrace and who is behind this.' The remark was left hanging with neither assent nor contradiction.

During the parliamentary debate, MP Antoni Szymanski set about embarrassing the Minister of Justice by asking him if he had 'failed to notice the tens of thousands of people who, over the past two years, had gone to kiosks and begged the assistants to cover it up, not to do this … You underestimate the efforts of people who took action to increase awareness in Poland on a massive scale, with no support from the law. And they proved effective, not the law…'

The ban and its handling were sharply criticised by most of the media, including the Catholic publications. A poll conducted by the Centre for the Study of Public Opinion put the question: 'Should all adults have the possibility of using magazines, video cassettes and other erotic materials if they wish, and should these materials therefore be available in Poland?' Seventy-two per cent of respondents answered 'yes'. Lawyers pointed out that it was unrealistic to try to ban pornography in the age of the free market and the Internet, and that it simply imitates authoritarian and totalitarian systems that punish for 'immorality'.

President Aleksander Kwasniewski vetoed the law on 27 March. It would need a two-thirds majority to override the veto and the right does not have that kind of majority in parliament. But the chances are that if the president had not used his veto, and the law had been implemented, not much would have changed. The lack of clear criteria plus the legal complications would have deterred the police and the public prosecutor's office from getting mixed up. The Poles are well versed in evading the rules, having done so very successfully throughout the latter years of communism.

But new enemies of Popper's 'Open Society' have appeared, new spokesmen for 'a healthy moral order' and new candidates for the job of censor. They are immensely energetic. The presidential veto infuriated right-wing politicians: MP Stefan Niesolowski called Kwasniewski 'the porn-president'. Kwasniewski was accused of counting on the support of

producers of pornography in his future campaigns for re-election.
Catholic media are constantly publishing protests to the president from
individuals and organisations containing an admixture of lament, insult
and threat; Radio Maria returns to the issue almost daily, presenting it as
a mortal threat to the nation; the Polish Federation of Movements for
the Defence of Life has already announced that it will 'take matters into
its own hands'.

The war against pornography is part of a bigger, considerably more
intricate picture. It isn't a case of a few fanatical groups stepping out into
the public eye. They have the support of large sectors of the population
who feel threatened and terrified by the new shape of the world,
liberalism, permissiveness, entry into the EU. They want resistance to
any innovation and a return to the old rules, including a strict control of
unfamiliar views and alien ways. ❑

Andrzej Oseka, an art critic and columnist with the Gazeta Wyborcza *in
Warsaw, contributed to the uncensored Polish press from 1982 to 1989.
Translated by Irena Maryniak*

MARCEL BERLINS

Disclosing innocence

**Non-disclosure of evidence has always formed part of the
English adversarial legal culture. That may finally be about to
change**

Under the English adversarial system of criminal justice, the vast
majority of the evidence relevant to a prosecution is gathered by
the police, and their main aim is to assemble enough of it to make a
conviction probable. Inevitably, in their pro-prosecution trawl, they
come across evidence which doesn't support the suspect's guilt; it may

actually go to proving his innocence. What should they do about it?

The principle, both moral and legal, is clear. The police – and the Crown Prosecution Service (CPS), which get the police's dossier and makes the final decision whether or not to prosecute – have a duty to disclose any relevant evidence which might be helpful to the accused. There's no dispute about the principle. All sides agree that it would be totally outrageous, and contrary to every tenet of a democratic system of justice, if important evidence in favour of an accused were secretly withheld in order to get a conviction. Putting those agreed ideals into practice, though, has not been successful, and miscarriages of justice caused by non-disclosure have continued, as a highly critical report of the Crown Prosecution Service Inspectorate – the independent body supervising the CPS – published in March 2000, makes clear.

The seriousness and frequency of the injustices resulting from non-disclosure came to light spectacularly in a series of cases in the late 1980s and early 1990s. Stephen Kiszko spent 16 years in prison for a murder and rape he could not have committed. His alleged victim had sperm inside her – yet there was medical evidence available to the prosecution at the time of his trial that he was physically incapable of producing sperm. Had the defence been told of this, there's little doubt he would have been acquitted. But they weren't – whether accidentally or deliberately is still not clear. Judith Ward was wrongly convicted of the M62 coach bombing, mainly because key evidence about her mental state at the time she was interviewed by the police wasn't made known to the defence. But for every high-profile miscarriage that becomes public, who knows how many unjust convictions resulting from non-disclosure have never been discovered?

An accused who is not told of evidence in his favour, which the prosecution know about, clearly cannot have a fair trial. So, for instance, if a prosecution witness has a criminal record, the defence will want to cross-examine him on it, to undermine his truthfulness; if a key witness has told conflicting stories in his statements to the police, that, too, is obvious ammunition for the defence. So is any ambivalent scientific evidence (the defence in the Maguire Seven trial wasn't told of the tests which failed to point to the defendants having touched explosives).

Until 1996, the prosecution's duty to disclose was governed by the Attorney-General's 1981 guidelines on 'unused material' – what the prosecution had, but weren't going to use in the trial. It didn't work because either the police or CPS genuinely didn't spot something which could help the defence, or (less often) deliberately didn't reveal it. They pointed out that, in some cases, the documentation runs into many thousands of pages, and hundreds of interviews have been conducted. The prosecution may know broadly what the accused's defence is to be, but they often don't know enough to realise what bits of evidence may or may not be pertinent. Sometimes, they add, when under the old system they gave the defence a list of the 'unused material' in their possession, the defence would demand to see a huge number of documents or listen to a large number of tapes. This defence scrutiny could take days – all at taxpayers' expense – and be little more than a fishing expedition, lawyers for an accused without a realistic defence desperately trying to find some small evidential crumb to use in court.

The Criminal Procedure and Investigations Act 1996 and its Code of Practice was meant to lay down new and clear guidelines for the prosecuting authorities, emphasising their duty to disclose 'unused material' which could – in the words of the statute – 'undermine the case for the prosecution against the accused', another way of saying help the defence. The Code sets out an elaborate procedure aimed at making sure that all material relevant to the investigation is properly kept and recorded. It also deals with exceptions to the duty to disclose, on the grounds that it's against the public interest to disclose the information, for example because it would reveal the name of an informant. This exception has long been controversial, even before the 1996 Act, with the defence in a number of cases claiming that they could not properly test the evidence of a witness whose identity had to be kept secret.

The CPS Inpectorate's March 2000 report found that the 1996 Act 'is not, at present, working as Parliament intended; nor does its present operation command the confidence of criminal practitioners. In a significant proportion of contested cases CPS compliance [with the Act] is defective in one or more respects; there is also uncertainty on the part of prosecutors about what is is expected of them'. While saying that the majority of cases are handled correctly, the report finds some fault with virtually every aspect of the way disclosure decisions are reached.

It's impossible to tell what miscarriages of justice may have occurred because of these weaknesses. The Inspectorate makes 33 recommendations for improvement. But what may be just as important as procedural reform is a change in prosecution culture. The newish

Director of Public Prosecutions David Calvert-Smith has made passionate promises of commitment to the cause of disclosure. If he gets his way, it will be good news for defendants in the dock – and for open justice. ❏

Marcel Berlins is presenter of BBC Radio 4's Law in Action and legal columnist of the Guardian. His book on the legal system, The Law Machine, (co-author Clare Dyer) is published by Penguin in July

NILOU MOBASSER

The last battle?

Threatened with the loss of power as the new, reform-minded parliament assembles in May, Iranian conservatives lash out

One might be forgiven for thinking the conservatives didn't like losing the first round of Iran's parliamentary elections on 18 February 2000. Imagine a football match in which, when one side realises it's going to lose badly, the players pull out guns and start shooting the players on the other side. Sa'id Hajjarian – a close ally of President Mohammad Khatami and managing director of the now-banned daily *Sobh-e Emrooz* (This Morning) as well as the strategist behind the reformists' electoral success – was shot in the face at point-blank range in broad daylight outside Tehran's city council offices on 12 March. The assailants used a type of motorcycle only available to the security forces; the guards outside the building did nothing to stop or apprehend the assailants. The failed assassination attempt was clearly intended to terrorise the public as much as to remove a brilliant rival from the field.

Since then, the reformists have suffered blow after blow including threatening statements by senior commanders of the *Pasdaran* (Islamic Revolution Guards Corps); moves by high-powered bodies – the Expediency Council headed by former presient Ali Akhbar Hashemi Rafsanjani and the Guardian Council – to limit the next parliament's prerogatives; the annulment and alteration of election results in about a dozen constituencies by the relevant supervisory body, the Guardian Council; endless delays by the same in announcing whether the Tehran election results–30 seats– have been endorsed or annulled; the hasty approval by the outgoing parliament of draconian changes to the Press Law; the imprisonment of some of the country's most respected journalists, including Mashallah Shamsolvaezin [*Index* 5/1998] and Akbar Ganji [*Index* 2/1998 (Index Index)]; and, as the *coup de grâce*, the banning of 16 reformist publications, including the dailies *Asr-e Azadegan* (Age of the Free Spirited, formerly know as *Jameah,* then *Tous,* then *Neshat* and now in its fourth incarnation after repeated bannings), *Fath* (Conquest), *Mosharekat* (Participation) and *Sobh-e Emrooz*; the weeklies *Aban* and *Ava* (Song); and the bi-monthly *Iran-e Farda* (Iran Tomorrow), in less than one week in April.

Although some observers have likened the situation to a coup, the description doesn't seem entirely apt in as much as the people who have 'seized' power already control the levers of power anyway. It would seem more accurate to say that, with their backs to the wall and their loss of control in the *majlis*, the power holders have simply gone berserk.

Normally, Iranian state television is extremely prudish, as one would expect in an 'Islamic Republic'. But in its determination to discredit the reformists, in mid-April, the conservative-controlled medium repeatedly broadcast edited clips from a conference on Iran at which a man took off all his clothes and a scantily dressed woman danced provocatively in the middle of the proceedings. The conference, held in Berlin on 7-9 April, was attended by intellectuals, writers and journalists from Iran – including Akbar Ganji – who had been invited by the Heinrich Böll Foundation to speak about the post-election situation in the country. The naked man and his dancing companion were opponents of the Islamic Republic living abroad and determined to disrupt the conference. However, as presented by Iranian TV, the conference itself revealed the shamelessness and immorality of the reformists. All the conference participants have subsequently been summoned for questioning by the Revolution Court, including the culture minister's wife and deputy-elect for Tehran, Jamileh Kadivar. Neither the culture minister's wife nor Kadivar has yet returned to Iran where arrest warrants await them on arrival. And three of the participants – Mehrangiz Kar, a lawyer who spoke about women's rights in Iran (or the lack thereof);

Shahla Lahiji, a publisher, who spoke about the problem of censorship; and student leader Ali Afshari, who was prevented from speaking at the conference by opposition intervention – were sent directly to prison after appearing before the Revolution Court some weeks after their return.

Meanwhile, in its zeal to close many of the country's most popular newspapers, the judiciary resorted to a law from the Shah's time that grants it preventative powers to detain 'repeat offenders and dangerous lunatics threatening public order'. Its bizarre recourse to this law made Iranian journalists comment bitterly that they probably were lunatics to attempt to publish newspapers in such difficult circumstances.

President Khatami, whose role carries little power in the system compared to other state insitutions, has reacted in perhaps the only way possible in the face of an opponent who lacks all restraint: he has appealed to the public to remain calm and wait for the new parliament to convene at the end of May. Together with the many journalists who have lost their jobs and the university students who were some of the banned publications' most avid readers, they have heeded the call. Students have held protest meetings and rallies throughout the country, but have remained on their campuses and not come out on to the streets. There are even reports that some students are beginning to publish makeshift campus newspapers to fill the vacuum. One piece of good news they might want to publish: despite the bullet lodged in his neck, Sa'id Hajjarian is recovering miraculously and has been released from hospital. ❏

Nilou Mobasser is an Iranian writer and translator based in the UK

MARK STEPHENS

Immune deficiency

British courts have allowed a libel action against Demon, a leading ISP. The result spells disaster for free expression on British-hosted websites, and has already prompted an online exodus to the free-speech territories of the US

The law does not render the owner of a house liable for defamatory words scrawled on the garage door by a third party, nor is the homeowner required to remove the words.

A telephone network operator is not liable for defamatory utterances transmitted across its network – even a recording played on a premium rate line. Operators are given immunity because they usually don't know what is said or, if they do, whether the words are defamatory. And, if defamatory, are they defensible?

Yet as British law stands, once notified that it is hosting defamatory material, an Internet Service Provider (ISP) is liable, even though it can have no knowledge as to the truth of the words complained of. Why are ISPs cast into such a different category of disseminator of alleged libels?

The answer lies in the blatant fudge reached in the drafting of section 1 of the Defamation Act 1996 in the protection to be given to 'innocent disseminators'. The 1996 review of the law – the first since 1952 – recognised the need to give a measure of protection to ISPs, but did not concede the full protection of immunity.

For libel to be established, an 'innocent disseminator' must know that defamatory material is being hosted, or believe that the material they host is of a character likely to contain defamatory material – the standard example of such charccter is the satirical magazine *Private Eye*. If not caught by either of those rules, if you are reckless as to whether you host defamatory material, the libel laws again catch you.

The UK approach is in stark contrast to that of the United States. The relevant law there is contained in the Communications Decency

Act 1996. This came under close judicial scrutiny as a result of the American Civil Liberties Union's challenge to its constitutionality in 1998. But one of the sections that withstood Supreme Court scrutiny was the immunity granted to ISPs.

The section was inserted to clarify the common law already developing. In *Cubby v CompuServe, 1995*, CompuServe successfully defeated a claim that it was responsible for defamatory statements appearing on a forum, 'Rumorville', accessible to its subscribers, but over which CompuServe had no control. In the same year, Prodigy Services Co were found liable for defamatory material it carried but, in this case, Prodigy was not independent of the bulletin board as it exercised editorial control.

Given the amount of content hosted by US ISPs, the legislature understood the impracticality of the court-imposed obligation to seek out defamatory material. The financial implications of rendering an ISP responsible for seeking out, and liable for, defamatory material was seen as a danger to the commercial viability of ISPs.

It was interesting and noteworthy that, when the same legislature came to consider the Digital Millennium Copyright Act, it determined not to afford the same immunity regarding copyright infringement as in defamation cases. Rather, it put in place a different scheme – a scheme that is now being advocated for ISPs in the UK in the absence of immunity. In effect, the safe harbour of immunity is given to ISPs who take the following prescribed steps:

notification to a specific addressee at a specific address;
ISP to remove offending words immediately;
communicate complaint to poster of offending words;
if the poster claims the words are not defamatory, they are put up again pending the outcome of any legal proceedings between defamer and defamed;
additional damages to be paid by poster to take account of the extra damage caused by putting the defamation back up.

This new approach avoids ISPs being targeted as 'deep pockets'. The litigation will be determined between the real protagonists – defamer and defamed – and not the owner of a virtual garage door. ❏

Mark Stephens is a senior partner with the London-based firm Finers Stephens Innocent and vice-chair of the Internet Watch Foundation

CHARLES ARTHUR

King Creole

Credit: Daniel Morel

Jean Dominique, Haiti's most prominent radio journalist and a passionate voice for democracy through decades of dictatorship and political turmoil, was shot dead by two gunmen outside his radio station in Port-au-Prince, Haiti's capital, on 3 April. He was 69 years old.

Dominique purchased the lease of Radio Haiti Inter, Haiti's oldest radio station, in 1968 and quickly began to revolutionise radio communications on the island. He pioneered the broadcasting of domestic as well as foreign news, and was the first to make use of eyewitness reports. His most revolutionary innovation was the conversion of news programming from French to Creole, the language of the majority. It made radio an accessible and influential medium for the first time.

Following an attack on Radio Haiti Inter by Papa Doc Duvalier's fearsome *Tontons Macoutes* in November 1980, Jean Dominique was forced into exile in the United States. The station reopened after the fall of Baby Doc Duvalier in 1986, but was closed down again when the military took power in October 1991. In 1995, Dominique restarted Radio Haiti Inter once more, resuming his fearless pursuit of the truth and genuine democratic change. ❏

Charles Arthur is a member of the Haiti Support Group

DAVID ROSENTHAL

Digital divides

A preparatory event for a UN conference against racism to be held next year heard controversial ideas proposed by a Swiss lawyer, designed to block racist websites. Detractors claim the proposals will establish a two-tier Internet

In 1998, the Swiss Federal Police tried to force Internet Service Providers (ISPs) to block access to certain racist websites abroad. The attempt failed and since then ISPs and the Swiss authorities have been trying, unsuccessfully, to find a solution to the problem that is acceptable on both sides.

While prosecution of Swiss ISPs for providing access to racist websites abroad still seems possible, it has become increasingly unrealistic and legally dubious. Also, at the moment, there seems to be no feasible, scalable technical solution that could limit access that doesn't itself pose new and more serious questions.

As a consequence, the focus has to shift to the source. If racist sites considered illegal are to be blocked, this has to happen at the point of origin, at the physical location where the sites are stored. In the case of racist websites, that is mostly in the US. Large service providers, like AOL, already take action against such sites on their own systems when they become aware of them. But racist groups can easily set up their own servers. This is true for non-US residents as well, as they can use US-based servers to spread propaganda. Under the banner of freedom of speech, the US has become the world's safe haven for racists.

If countries where such material is illegal are to do anything about it, they must find new ways to address the issue. Whether the actions discussed here and in the full report are wise, politically opportune and realistic is another question; this article shall only put forward ideas. However, it is clear that solving the problem will require the co-operation of the ISP community at source, rather than the ones at the end of the chain.

In the US, it is not legally possible to prohibit providers from carrying racist material. On the other hand, US providers, in most cases, are not legally obliged to host racist content either. Knowing this, some countries or groups could start to put pressure on those providers to voluntarily stop supporting such content. A commercial ISP knowingly and willingly assisting in the overseas publication of illegal racist material can, for example, already be prosecuted in some European countries, if they have operations there. Many service providers operate on an international basis, surely few would want to risk facing court action in countries where they want to do business. Even the threat of legal action has been successful in forcing American companies to take notice of foreign law. German authorities were able to put sufficient pressure on Amazon to stop it selling *Mein Kampf* to German customers. And when the EU threatened legal action against US firms that flout new data protection laws in their European operations, the US was forced to work out measures acceptable for both sides, which has lead to the adoption of a 'Safe Harbour' concept.

Another option would be to put pressure on Internet domain registration bodies, which administer website addresses, to withdraw names from racist groups – effectively kicking them out of the Internet. This example also makes clear that new 'solutions' might be effective and attractive, but can also be abused.

In this regard 'self-regulation' is frequently called upon. But the thorny issues – deciding what content should actually be blocked – remain in place, and the decision-makers have even less democratic justification than governments and courts. In the US, a handful of vendors of censorware already decide what can be accessed in many schools, libraries and other public offices.

There also is a danger that anti-democratic regimes could use censorware to suppress free speech on the pretext of fighting racism. Ultimately, it's a question of what should and should not be tolerated on a network that covers thousands of diverging cultural ideologies. The answer may well be to set a minimum standard, somewhat of a compromise between countries that outlaw racism and those that take a more liberal line.

If racism on the Internet is to be challenged, it must be done with a combination of governmental control and self-regulation, whereby compromise becomes a requirement, not merely a possibility. Content owners could for example be required to at least tag their information in a machine-readable format which would ease filtering where required.

ISPs in countries such as the US could also work towards ensuring that racist content on US servers can only be accessed by a US audience. This is possible with reasonable efforts by using certain Internet protocol information.

Such a system would also provide protection against prosecution for all participants (even the authors) without limiting freedom of speech in countries not willing to do so. US companies used similar techniques to prevent foreign downloads of software containing strong encryption. The judgment on what constitutes an acceptable website content could be transferred to an internationally recognised body. This – not technology – remains the hard part. ❏

David Rosenthal *(rosenthal@insider.ch) works as a legal and IT counsel for governments, industry and several international organisations, and as a lecturer at the University of Basel law school. The full text of this report can be found at www.rvo.ch/docs/unracism.pdf*
Translated by Syra Morley

The privacy issue

Corporations and governments alike cite privacy as a defence for censorship. Yet freedom of speech and privacy are both recognised as human rights – how can a balance be struck? Who are the enemies of privacy? And, in a wired future, will any of us have a private life?

File compiled by Frank Fisher

SIMON DAVIES

Private matters

A grey and featureless office building in Edinburgh is currently playing host to one of the most extraordinary episodes in the ancient struggle between individual privacy and the power of the state. Here, in the headquarters of the Lothian and Borders Police, the DNA of the local population is being systematically archived.

For the past two years, every person arrested or detained by Edinburgh police has been forced to submit to a DNA test. The offences that warrant this practice are not confined to the obvious categories of murder, rape and burglary, but also to traffic offences, shoplifting, and public order transgressions such as breach of the peace.

In terms of privacy, the Edinburgh policy is momentous. The collection and storage of DNA must surely rank as one of the most intimate invasions of the person, and yet a recent opinion poll suggests that nearly three-quarters of the local population would be willing to give up their DNA in the 'pursuit of a crime'.

The police are unwilling to concede that the practice has implications for civil rights. One spokesperson recently told the BBC 'bear in mind that the person committing a traffic offence might be a major criminal, and this is our chance to capture his DNA and identify him'.

It is still too early to figure whether the programme has achieved real success, but Prime Minister Tony Blair has already signalled that he wants all UK police forces to follow the Edinburgh policy.

The Home Office and other government agencies have also been excited by the potential of DNA testing. Recent Child Support Agency legislation requires all alleged runaway fathers to submit to a DNA test. Failure to do so is tantamount in law to an admission of guilt. It is likely that within a generation, the DNA of most of the UK population will have been archived in a national database.

The current mania for DNA testing goes to the heart of the privacy

issue. Traditionally, invasion of privacy has been justified on the basis of effective social management. Police have always argued that privacy and anonymity are bad news for law enforcement. Authority has always sought to create perfect identification of citizens. And DNA is the perfect identifier.

But the popularity of DNA testing is merely a symptom of a much broader trend. Governments and private sector organisations have moved in recent years to incorporate surveillance into almost every aspect of our finances, communication and lifestyle. They argue that surveillance is necessary to maintain law and order and to create economic efficiency. The rationale is often self-serving, and somewhat bogus, but a substantial number of people have nevertheless been persuaded that the surrender of privacy is the price we must pay for a better and safer society.

The issue has never been simple. The protection of individual privacy has always been one of the great polemics of human rights. At its heart is a struggle to find the ideal balance between the autonomy of the individual, and the power of the state. With each new intrusion into private life – be it closed circuit television surveillance (CCTV), email monitoring or direct marketing – people are obliged to make choices between their individual rights and the rights of society.

Whether through cause or effect, privacy now occupies an unenviable place in the catalogue of human rights. Along with censorship and free speech, privacy defies resolution. And yet, as one writer has observed, 'privacy is the right from which all other rights derive'. It is central to the freedom and autonomy of people, and it is perhaps the key factor that limits the power of the state.

There has never been a time when so much information has been amassed on the population at large. Details of economically active adults in the developed world are located in around 400 major databases – enough processed data to compile a formidable reference book for each person. Electronic visual surveillance in urban centres is almost ubiquitous. Nearly all forms of electronic communication are now routinely scanned and profiled. In the past, surveillance was based on the targeting of specific individuals or groups. Now, systematic surveillance pro-actively profiles millions of people at a time.

Public reaction to privacy invasion has been contradictory and unpredictable. In the United States, the fingerprinting of welfare recipients has proceeded with scarcely a murmur of protest, while in Australia, attempts by the federal government to introduce a national identity card sparked the biggest public protest in living memory. Yet while Australian legislation forcing banks to report suspicious transactions passed without notice, similar legislation in the US provoked more than a quarter of a million written complaints.

Torture, discrimination, racial hatred: these issues have achieved baseline consensus within the international community. Privacy, however, is viewed by many individuals, governments and corporations as the bogeyman of human rights. It is conventional wisdom among many organisations that privacy of the individual and the protection of personal information impedes economic performance and law enforcement.

The result is that many countries are becoming surveillance societies. The justification is seductive and difficult to oppose. And in our quite innocent and natural desire to save a few pounds, or just to be good citizens, we yield information constantly about our finances, purchases, employment, interests, telephone activity and even our movements. When we do so, organisations are ready to exploit the data. Surveillance has become a fixed component of the burgeoning information economy.

The power, capacity and speed of information technology are accelerating rapidly. The extent of privacy invasion – or the potential to invade privacy – increases correspondingly. Globalisation of systems such as the Internet removes geographical limitations (and legal protections) to the flow of data. Convergence is leading to the elimination of technological barriers between systems.

I recently presented a BBC documentary on privacy, in which I described one of the unforeseen results of these macro-trends in technology. UK InfoDisc has produced a CD-ROM which merges the electoral roll with the telephone book and geodemographic data. So now the most basic and innocent information about you can reveal all manner of additional facts. Your telephone number leads instantly to your address. Your name leads automatically to your occupation and age. It goes without saying that the finance and credit industry, private investigators, newspapers, marketing companies and police all make extensive use of the product.

These issues are important because the increasing informational bond between citizen and state (and of course the private sector) diminishes human autonomy. As decision-making by government agencies, banks and insurance companies becomes automated, the factors that affect our lives are made on the basis of an increasing mass of personal data.

In developing countries, the threat is magnified. The perfect identification of individuals can have fatal consequences. Governments of developing nations rely on First World countries to supply them with technologies of surveillance such as digital wiretapping equipment, deciphering equipment, scanners, bugs, tracking equipment and computer intercept systems. This transfer is now a lucrative sideline for the arms industry. A report published in 1995 by my organisation,

Privacy International, highlighted the extent of the trade.

The report analysed the companies that export to developing countries with a poor human rights record, finding that: 'The surveillance trade is almost indistinguishable from the arms trade. More than 70% of companies manufacturing and exporting surveillance technology also export arms, chemical weapons or military hardware. Surveillance is a crucial element for the maintenance of any non-democratic infrastructure, and an important activity in the pursuit of intelligence and political control.'

This analysis was supported by a 1997 report, *Assessing the Technologies of Political Control*, commissioned by the European Parliament's Civil Liberties Committee from the European Commission's Science and Technology Options Assessment office (STOA).

According to the STOA report, much of this technology is used to track the activities of dissidents, human rights activists, journalists, student leaders, minorities, trade union leaders and political opponents. The view that surveillance technology is inherently hostile to individual rights was articulated with some vehemence. The document cast several categories of information technology – ID systems, biometric technology, wiretapping systems, etc – in a negative light, linking their implementation to the denial of basic human rights, concluding that such technologies can exert a powerful 'chill effect' on those who 'might wish to take a dissenting view, and few will risk exercising their right to democratic protest'. As Privacy International observed: 'In the absence of meaningful legal or constitutional protections, such technology is inimical to democratic reform. It can certainly prove fatal to anyone "of interest" to a regime.'

While IT companies routinely promote their technologies as a means of achieving social reform, the human rights community increasingly defines them as a means of social and political control.

CCTV may turn out to be the most obvious – and onerous – future intrusion. CCTV systems have moved in the space of 15 years from 'first generation' (stand alone cameras) to 'second generation' (the networking of cameras through telecommunications systems) to the modern 'third generation' systems that are integrated with software to automatically recognise faces and to analyse individual behaviour. In Britain, hundreds of thousands of cameras have been placed into buses, trains, lifts and even phone booths. Hidden cameras – once frowned on – are now being installed unhindered in cinemas, police helmets, pubs, red-light districts, changing rooms and housing estates. Forget the cumbersome technology portrayed in *1984*. It is the integration of CCTV with the environment that is most telling.

Visual surveillance in Britain is becoming a fixed component in the design of modern urban centres, new housing areas, public buildings and even throughout the road system (a massive network of linked numberplate recognition cameras will bring an end to anonymity on the road within ten years). Soon, people will expect spy technology to be engineered into all forms of architecture and design. It is, perhaps, only a matter of time before legal and community pressures force the cameras into our homes.

The ubiquity of visual surveillance will be paralleled by mass surveillance of Internet and telephone activity. US and European law enforcement agencies have already laid the foundations for a massive eavesdropping system capable of intercepting all mobile phones, Internet communications, fax messages and pagers throughout Europe. The plan, known as ENFOPOL 98, has been drawn up in secret by police and government officials as part of a Europe-wide strategy to create a 'seamless' web of telecommunications surveillance.

Privacy activists are struggling to block ENFOPOL 98, which is being promoted using the dirtiest of tactics. At a recent Russian conference on Internet rights, Austrian campaigner Erich Moechel released official summary documents from international police working groups that clearly indicate that authorities intend to exploit public concern about child pornography as a 'strategy' to promote efforts to place the Internet under surveillance 'even though these issues are not neccessarily relevant'.

ENFOPOL, which has received widespread support in the EU Justice and Home Affairs Council – Europe's peak policing body – will oblige all ISPs (Internet Service Providers) and telephone exchanges to provide agencies with 'real time, full time' access to all communications, regardless of the country of origin. All new communications media, including interactive cable television, will also be required to provide full access to law enforcement agencies.

The ENFOPOL strategy will be aided by a 'subject tagging' system capable of tracking targets wherever they travel. Known as the 'International User Requirements for Interception' (IUR), the tagging system, which is currently being designed, will create a data processing and transmission network which involves not only the names, addresses and phone numbers of targets and associates, but email addresses, credit-card details, PINs and passwords. The system will also merge mobile phone data to create a comprehensive geographic location tracking system.

ENFOPOL is just one of several burgeoning systems used to track and profile international communications. Perhaps the most astounding system is ECHELON, a global eavesdropping system established by the US National Security Agency. This system was designed to operate in the core of international telecommunications systems, and can sift through tens of millions of emails and faxes to discover keywords of interest to the United States and its allies (*Index* 5/98).

In the UK, the Regulation of Investigatory Powers Bill (an exact parallel of Russia's controversial SORM Bill), currently in its third reading, will provide the government with an armoury of powers to place computer and Internet use under surveillance. The measures have the potential effect of criminalising encryption users (and that, ultimately, means any future computer use). The Bill also gives authorities the right, without the requirement of a warrant, to monitor information on Internet traffic. That is, which websites you visited, who you have been emailing, and which newsgroups you visit.

Tax and revenue authorities will in the future use the Bill to conduct a massive driftnet fishing operation over the entire Internet, analysing and profiling the activities of millions of Internet users.

Perfect surveillance requires perfect identity, and the next 20 years will see a comprehensive effort by authorities to achieve this end. As well as establishing widespread DNA testing, government agencies and businesses are likely to introduce systems of electronic finger- and hand-scanning systems.

These systems, known as 'biometric identifiers' are already in use throughout the world. They claim to produce near perfect identification of the individual by electronically scanning the fine details of a hand, finger or even eye.

Spain has a national fingerprint system for unemployment benefit and healthcare entitlement. Russia has announced plans for a national electronic fingerprint system for banks. Jamaicans are required to scan their thumbs into a database before qualifying to vote at elections. In

France and Germany, tests are under way with equipment that puts fingerprint information on to credit cards. The technology is being used by retail outlets, government agencies, childcare centres, police forces and automated-teller machines. Microsoft recently announced that it will incorporate biometrics into its new operating systems to aid Internet security.

For the past five years, the US Immigration and Naturalization Service (INS) has been developing an automated passport control system using hand geometry. In this project, frequent travellers have their hand geometry stored in a 'smart' card. The traveller places their hand on to a scanner, and places the card into a slot. More than 70,000 people have enrolled in the trial. A spokesman for the INS recently told the *Daily Telegraph* that the organisation intends to create a worldwide biometric system for travellers.

But it will be the growth of surveillance in the workplace that will most directly affect people. Workers in most countries have almost no right to privacy. Employers are permitted – 'within reason' – to place all employees under constant surveillance. They can tap phones, read email and monitor computer screens. They can bug conversations, analyse computer and keyboard work, peer through CCTV cameras, use tracking technology to monitor personal movements, analyse urine to detect drug use, and demand the disclosure of intimate personal data, The casualisation of the workforce accelerates these activities.

Telephone software such as WatCall from Harlequin analyses the calls made and received by employees. In computer- and telephone-based industries, such software packages have turned supervisors into the digital equivalent of Victorian workhouse foremen. It's likely that any manager who purchases network-operating software is already getting built-in eavesdropping functions. Some packages, such as Win Watch Professional and Norton-Lambert's Close-Up/LAN software, allow network administrators to observe an employee's screen in real time, scan data files and email, and analyse keystroke performance.

Even your home will not be free from surveillance. Consider the example of the new generation of interactive digital television services coming on stream. These products offer a new intimacy between TV service provider and customer. By directly drawing information on customers' viewing habits, financial transactions and on-screen 'vox pop' surveys, the company can create a complex profile of every customer.

US researcher David Burke found that, in the words of UK information analyst William Heath, digital TV creates 'full experimental conditions in every user home, with a measurable cycle of stimulus, measurement and response'.

Privacy is eroded in countless other ways. Mobile phones are being turned into geographical tracking devices. The Internet has become a means to profile and analyse the behaviour and habits of its users. In an ideal world, such techniques should be counter-balanced by the use of technologies and laws that protect privacy, but the trend internationally has been for governments to inhibit the spread of privacy-friendly technologies such as encryption, and to pass legislation that mandates surveillance.

However, the most dangerous enemy of privacy is not an interior minister or marketing supremo; it is the well-meaning individual who argues: 'I have nothing to hide, so I have nothing to fear.' Nothing could be further from the truth. Everyone has a sphere of private life which must be protected from intrusion. Few people could honestly claim that their life – their family details, financial affairs and health history – is an open book. Even if this was so, their happy position should not provide a rationale for the invasion of other people's lives.

But the argument for privacy goes well beyond the integrity and autonomy of each individual. Privacy is the fundamental test of the strength of a free society. The right to privacy is the right to protect ourselves against intrusion by the outside world. It is the measure we use to set limits on the demands made upon us. It is the right we invoke to defend our personal freedom, our autonomy and our identity. It is the basis upon which we assess the balance of power between ourselves and the world around us.

Privacy is the natural partner of freedom of expression. They are equal and compatible rights. Moreover, both have evolved in the modern context as a synergy. As the world embraces the information society, and as our lives go increasingly online, the forces which promote censorship also diminish privacy – and vice versa. It will become apparent in the coming years that these two rights will form the great pillars of any free society. ❏

Simon Davies *is the director general of Privacy International,* www.privacy.org/pi, *and a fellow at the London School of Economics*

STEPHEN GRAHAM

The fifth utility

An initiative begun in Britain is taking hold across the developed world: building CCTV into construction plans is becoming as normal as incorporating running water

'You're under CCTV surveillance' signs are everywhere these days. But these might soon be replaced by signs that say 'Warning! You are entering an area which is NOT covered by CCTV!'

So widespread is CCTV coverage becoming, and so reliant are we on the gaze of millions of electronic eyes, that we may soon start to treat the absence or collapse of CCTV systems with the same fear and anxiety with which we treat electricity cuts or the collapse of the phone network. We might soon have a fear of unwatched spaces. CCTV, in short, looks set to become a fifth utility, to join electricity, gas, water and telephone networks as ubiquitous infrastructures that we expect to cover all places and therefore largely take for granted.

How can we tell that CCTV is on the verge of omnipresence? I would point to four early signs. The first and simplest is its widening geographical coverage. CCTV now covers so many of our town and city centres, shopping malls, petrol stations, leisure centres, stadia, car parks, transport networks and residential and public spaces that soon virtually every part of our waking hours will be spent under surveillance.

In 1999, 500 British towns and cities had public CCTV systems – up from 74 in 1996 – and the expansion rate is remarkable. The British CCTV market is currently the biggest in Europe at over £385m (US$616M) per year.

Once established, CCTV systems generally add cameras to cover larger areas on a continuous basis to make the most of the investment in people and technology. Within cities like Newcastle-upon-Tyne, for example, separate systems now cover the city centre, main shopping malls, district centres, business parks, transport networks, stadia and a growing range of housing and residential districts. The uncovered space between these areas is diminishing fast.

Beyond the main towns and cities, there is a notable shift of CCTV towards smaller and more remote rural areas. Smaller settlements, worried by fear of crime and potential overspill from urban areas with CCTV, are installing their own systems. In Wales, a progressive diffusion has led to Cardigan, with 4,000 people, and Newcastle Emlyn, with 1,500, now having CCTV.

The second sign is that the growth of CCTV is fuelling itself in a spiral of self-reinforcement. This is happening through its symbiotic relationship with television. More and more of the world's criminal acts are caught directly on camera. Soon after, they are beamed direct to our living rooms through the countless news reports and cheap crime shows that flood TV, from *Police Stop!* to *America's Dumbest Criminals.* Even local newspapers are now keen to print CCTV images of convicted criminals' faces. The deputy editor of one such paper, the *Portsmouth Evening News*, believes this is 'part of what makes CCTV effective'. Ade Thomas, a former researcher for the civil liberties group Liberty, argues that this close connection between TV, local news and CCTV is accelerating the shift to ubiquitous surveillance. Viewers react to crime shows by developing further anxieties about the risks of crime. In response to these anxieties, they are likely to support the extension of CCTV. Thus, more and more crime events will be captured to be relayed on to TV programmes. And so the spiral continues.

The third sign is more subtle. Over the past few years, attention in the British media has started to shift from watched places to unwatched ones. As part of this process of what sociologists call 'normalisation', every murder, school break-in or terrorist act intensifies the demands for surveillance. The question, especially in the local and tabloid press, has shifted from 'Are these new CCTV schemes a good thing?' to 'Why can't we have cameras everywhere?'

Take a couple of examples. The recent installation of CCTV in Chapeltown, Leeds, was prompted by the murder there of Stefan Popvich in 1996. Local councillors were criticised for not installing the system before the murder, to either deter it or help detect the culprit. And when cameras were removed from Ladyton shopping centre in Scotland a few months before a murder there in 1996, the local press reported this 'video blunder' in more detail than the murder itself.

It seems the newsworthy events emerge not when another CCTV system is installed or when CCTV images are used by the police or private security personnel. Rather, media and public attention is on the dangers and threats that lurk in unwatched places, either when camera systems fail, or when serious crime occurs in the interstitial, uncovered spaces between existing CCTV systems.

The final ominous sign of the shift to ubiquitous surveillance comes from the remarkable technological changes under way. CCTV is starting to be computerised. This shift to digital CCTV will have two crucial consequences. First, it will remove barriers to geographical expansion. This is because digital CCTV systems can be programmed to automatically search for specified events and people within much larger systems than are currently possible, rather than relying on the built-in limits of the 'Mk1 eyeball' of the human operator. Second, it is very easy to link computerised CCTV to databases of car registration plates and human faces. In other words, technologies for crude visual tracking quickly become automatic tracking systems which can memorise movements in time and space as well as tracking them in 'real time'.

In digital CCTV systems, computer programmes stipulate what an 'unusual' event is – say a person running, loitering, or the presence of a specified individual or car. It then sets the cameras recording, and may signal an alert to human operators. Early trials for these sorts of technologies are already in operation, with Britain leading the world. London's financial district, the City, is encircled by cameras that automatically scan car registration plates, linking instantaneously to the computerised records of the Driver & Vehicle Licencing Centre (DVLC). Suspect vehicles, or cars moving the 'wrong way' down a street automatically trigger alerts. Alerts sound if cars entering the zone do not leave within a specified time.

In 1999, the east London borough of Newham introduced a system that actively scans for the 'target faces' of 600–1,000 habitual and suspected criminals, 24 hours a day through 140 fixed and 11 mobile cameras using a software system called Mandrake. The software is based on a sophisticated 'neural network' programme, that analyses and learns in a similar way to the human brain.

But the real potential for linking databases to digital CCTV will come when local CCTV networks start to interconnect into bigger, national or even international systems. With an effective national CCTV

CCTV control room – Credit: Terry Williams/Rex

system it will be very simple for law enforcement bodies to track the movements of *all* cars and people continuously and in real time.

Long-mooted national identity cards might in the future provide a comprehensive database of the population's photographs, although even now passport agency records have been digitised, and all new driving licences will require a digitised photograph. However it develops, those who are not registered within the system – illegal immigrants, for example – will be easy to isolate as 'unknowns' within databases, and then track. Movements, activities and behaviours might be archived to support later analysis of 'suspicious' activities. And incidences of crime might be correlated with people's movements to identify suspects through 'proactive policing'.

Paradoxically, CCTV will become less rather than more visible in this shift towards ubiquitous surveillance. Cameras with lenses mounted directly on to printed circuit boards already measure little more than an inch across. Every year the trend is for smaller and cheaper cameras. They will also become deliberately covert. But in fact the very ubiquity of the cameras will render them so utterly banal that few will bother to take much notice (the way we treat phones and electricity sockets now). Soon we will begin to assume that they are there, embedded in everything from lamp-posts to clocks, doors, street lights and bus stops.

These trends seem convincing. The CCTV industry itself recognises the likely emergence of a nationally integrated CCTV infrastructure for real-time face and car tracking, forged out of the gradual merging of thousands of individual CCTV 'islands'. Jon Fassenbender, a commentator in *CCTV Today* magazine, admitted recently that the full usefulness of CCTV and facial recognition will only come 'when a national database is established to provide instant image analysis'. At the moment, public opinion would probably support such a scheme, but as Fassenbender himself points out, changing circumstances may force a rethink: 'At the moment, CCTV is very much flavour of the month. But what might happen in perhaps ten years' time when most individual surveillance systems have been gradually integrated towards providing total coverage, as part of a larger, integrated scheme?' ❏

Dr Stephen Graham *works at the Centre for Urban Technology at Newcastle University. A version of this article previously appeared in* Environment and Planning B *(1999)*

CLIVE NORRIS & GARY ARMSTRONG

Space invaders

In theory CCTV operates fairly and responsibly, helping to uphold the law without prying into innocent lives. The reality of a CCTV control room in northern England raises the old question: 'Who guards the guards?'

14.00: While surfing the cameras and streets the operators see two young men standing in a pedestrian shopping precinct, both looking into a holdall bag one of them is carrying. While this scene is not remarkable, what is unusual is that one of the two is black, a rare sight in the city centre. The two are in their early 20s and smartly dressed. After a minute or so, one hands to the other a piece of paper which most onlookers would presume was an address or phone number. Finally, on going their separate ways the two indulge in a fashionable 'high-five' handshake. This alerts both operators.

To these two, the 'high-five' was suspicious because it was not done with flathands and it 'wasn't firm enough'. In fact, according to the second operator, one of the men had a distinctly cupped band. While this was explainable by his holding the piece of paper just given him by the other, the operators see only criminality – this could be a surreptitious, yet overtly public exchange of drugs. The youth with the bag is surveilled closely as he continues his walk. He not only has a bag, possibly the merchandise, but he is also black – a drug dealer. The suspect then enters a men's fashion store which means that the camera is now trained on the doors while the operator awaits a possible hasty reappearance complete with stolen items in shoulder bag. After a few minutes, the camera is zoomed into the store and the suspect is visible in a capacity the operators did not consider – he is a sales assistant.

01.00: On the first nightshift the operator is keen to show me all his job entails. Eventually I am taken, via the camera, to 'Shaggers Alley', an area of a car park near the railway station which is the most discreet town centre place for punters who have picked up prostitutes soliciting from an adjacent industrial estate about a mile away. While this location is out of the way to passers-by many a punter, and indeed a happy couple not involved in a financial transaction, are unaware of the reach of the all-seeing camera whose job is facilitated by a large and powerful car-park light which does not leave much to the imagination of the observer.

Clearly visible on this night, thanks to the cameras' ability to zoom in and look into cars, is a male in his late 20s sitting in the driver's seat with what can only be described as an expression of glee as a female, kneeling on the passenger seat performs fellatio on him. Her hair and head are noticeably bouncing up and down for around two minutes. When the performance is over the woman is clearly visible topless in the front seat. From beginning to end this scenario is put on to the police monitor, the operator informing me that the police officers in the communications office enjoy such scenarios and when bored will sometimes phone to ask him to put the cameras on Shaggers Alley for their titillation.

01.05: The operator notices a couple in the street having an animated row. Both are white and in their late 20s and stylishly dressed as if returning from a night out. This quiet Monday night has produced nothing of interest and these two arguing is the most interesting event of the past three hours. This and the fact that the woman in view is blonde and good-looking has added to the attraction and so the operator tells the police control-room staff (two men) to have a look at the event unfolding.

After a two-minute argument the woman storms off up the street, but does not go out of the man's sight and slumps against a wall looking miserable. The man, meanwhile, climbs into a nearby car, closes the door and waits in the driver's seat, lights off. The impasse lasts five minutes, the female walks slowly towards the car and begins to talk to the man via the driver's window, only to storm off again after a minute. This time the male follows her on foot to continue the row. The operators and police enter into a commentary urging the man not to chase after her and having decided she is hot-tempered and sulky the operator says aloud: 'You hit her and we'll be your witnesses.'

The couple continue their debate and this time the female decides to walk off past the man, but as she does so he attempts to restrain her by holding her arm. She pulls back. In the stand-off, further words are exchanged and a blow is aimed from the male to the female which strikes her around the upper chest and causes her to stumble. The blow does not look to be a hard one and she picks herself up and walks away. Meanwhile, the male returns to his car and once again sits and waits. This time the female walks down the street past the car and continues for 20 yards only to stop, walk back to the car and stand looking into it.

After a couple of minutes of her looking and him pretending not to notice, the pair resume their chat, this time via the passenger door. The drama continues when she walks away again, this time the distance is only ten yards, then she does an about-turn, opens the front passenger door and while she sits in it, she leaves the door wide open. After a mutual silence (seen by zooming the camera into the car's windscreen), the pair decide to talk again. This time she lasts three minutes before getting out and storming off.

By now, other police personnel have appeared to watch this drama. Two other officers have entered the room so that six men can now, in pantomime mode, boo and cheer good moves and bad moves. One boo is reserved for the male when he starts up the car, does a three-point turn and drives up to where she is sulking and tries to persuade her to get in. A cheer goes up when he has seemingly failed in this effort and so drives away. But cheers turn to boos when he reverses to resume his persuasion. His words work and, to boos from her audience, she climbs in the car and after a four-minute discussion the stationary car drives away into the distance. ❏

Clive Norris is senior lecturer in criminology, at the Centre For Criminology and Criminal Justice, University of Hull. *Gary Armstrong* is jecturer in sociology and criminology, at the University of Reading. These extracts are taken from The Maximum Surveillance Society *(Berg, 1999)*

DAVID BANISAR

Big browser is watching you

In the US, the rapid development of Internet technologies, combined with a lack of legal protections for privacy, is turning the Internet into the World Wide Watcher. Controversy is growing but there is little action from government

'You have zero privacy – get over it!' Scott McNealy, CEO, Sun Microsystems.

The use of personal information as a commodity which is collected by corporations with little regard for the privacy of individuals has reached epidemic proportions. The law has lagged behind as companies and government agencies oppose new protections and demand greater access to information for commercial and law enforcement purposes.

This information ranges from the trivial to the most sensitive. It includes financial records, medical records, details of reading habits, political opinions, sexual interests and other data that most people consider private. Much of this information is routinely collected by computers connected to the Internet.

The misuse of information is behind the stock-market valuation of many dotcom companies. They gather personal information from visitors by offering personalised services such as news searches, free email and stock portfolios. They then sell that information to advertisers or allow advertisers to access market segments. It is then repurposed by government agencies, companies and individuals for any number of uses ranging from unsolicited email (known as spam) to checking job references, targeting advertising and conducting criminal investigations. Banks use the information in a practice called 'weblining' to determine who to give service to and which customers to drop.

According to Forrester Research, nearly a quarter of US companies are using information gathered from the Internet to develop detailed profiles of customers. Some are going after the youth market. ZapMe loans computers and a satellite link to schools then collects the names, addresses and phone numbers of students and transfers that information to corporate sponsors.

Other information, such as credit records, that was formerly available only to professionals such as private detectives, is now available to anyone with a credit card. In September 1999, 20-year-old Amy Boyer was gunned down after a stalker used two information brokers to obtain her New Hampshire address.

The most controversial area has been the identification of net users. Most users believe that they are anonymous as they browse the net but in reality they leave behind information trails that can be used to identify them. Companies have been developing new ways to improve identification and merge user identities with real names and personal information. The most pervasive tracking technology is the cookie.

The cookie is a small file containing a serial number that is placed on a user's hard drive by a website. Cookies were developed to improve websites' ability to track users over a session. The cookie can also notify the site that the user has returned and can allow the site to track the user's habits across many different visits. The use of cookies expanded greatly when it was realised that a single cookie could be used by many different sites. This led to the development of advertising network companies that can track users across thousands of sites.

The largest ad service is DoubleClick, which has agreements with over 11,000 websites and maintains cookies on 100 million users, each linking to hundreds of pieces of information about the user's browsing habits. In 1999, DoubleClick announced that it was buying Abacus, owner of the largest direct marketing lists in the country with information on the purchasing habits of 90% of all US households, and that DoubleClick was going to merge information from the purchasing databases with information from online browsing. Following criticism, the Federal Trade Commission and several state attorney generals are challenging the merger of the information without the consent of the users.

Not satisfied with cookies, which can be deleted by a user, the computer industry is now trying permanent methods of identifying users. In 1999, Intel announced that it was including a serial number in each new Pentium III chip that could be accessed by websites and internal corporate networks. Most of the manufacturers suppressed the number after a consumer boycott was announced. Meanwhile, Microsoft and RealAudio were caught using the internal networking number found in most computers as another identifier.

The Internet Engineering Task Force has developed specifications for the next version of the Internet's underlying protocols called IPv6 that will assign a unique permanent ID number to every device hooked into the net – one day including your refrigerator and VCR. Who needs cookies when your refrigerator will inform on you?

Other companies are trying a different approach, offering to become 'information brokers'. Under many of these systems, the users provide information to the company who then provide it to the third-party website with the consent of the user. Many of these systems, such as Microsoft's Passport and the World Wide Web Consortium's (W3C) Platform for Privacy Preferences (P3P), are designed more to facilitate data sharing than to protect users. They are also frequently used by industry as justification for not passing laws.

Internet security also raises serious problems for privacy. In April 2000, it was revealed that an unknown Microsoft engineer had included a backdoor into its webserver software. If someone typed 'Netscape engineers are weenies!' backwards, they would have full control of websites and associated data. De Beers lost 35,000 names, addresses, phone numbers and email addresses of people inquiring about buying diamonds following a security breach in March.

To respond to these challenges, many countries are adopting new laws. The European Union enacted two data protection directives in 1995 and 1997 to extend privacy protections. Nearly 40 countries have comprehensive laws or are in the process of adopting them. However, the US government refuses to accept these international standards.

The official policy of the US government is to oppose privacy laws and to promote industry self-regulation. In limited areas, it supports sectoral laws. For instance, there are laws that cover records generated by video rentals and ensure the privacy of some email. The only solid law that has passed on Internet privacy covered the collection of information on children under the age of 13.

Perhaps the biggest difference between the European approach and that in the US is the lack of a government body that provides for oversight and enforcement. The US Federal Trade Commission has a very limited jurisdiction over 'false and deceptive practices'. Activists describe the agency as weak and ineffective. Each year, it conducts a survey of privacy policies of websites that it always finds inadequate but then calls again for industry self-regulation.

The industry also promotes self-regulatory bodies TrustE and BBB Online which give out 'seals' to reassure net users that the sites support privacy. However, these bodies receive large amounts of money from the companies they are supposed to oversee, and have yet to sanction any company for any privacy violation. TrustE has refused to deal with several issues against Microsoft, Intel and RealAudio.

To respond to the EU Data Protection Directive, the US Department of Commerce proposed creating a 'Safe Harbour' for US companies to continue to work with European partners without adequate legislation. Under the agreement, US companies voluntarily agree to follow a set of privacy principles more in keeping with EU standards. With nothing to defend EU data in the hands of US companies except self-regulation, European privacy and consumer groups are considering suing if the agreement is approved.

The endless list of privacy scandals has led to a growing backlash as consumer and privacy groups have organised campaigns and boycotts. Company stock prices have been crushed when new abuses appear. Lawyers have filed class-action suits based on computer crime laws against companies such as RealAudio for violating privacy. Several companies have backed down from their controversial proposals and government agencies, especially on state level, are starting to investigate company practices. However, the lack of a federal agency to protect privacy has hampered these efforts. In Congress, two privacy caucuses have been set up. Several hundred bills have been introduced in the last two sessions but in the face of massive industry donations and lobbying, not one Internet privacy bill has advanced. ❏

David Banisar is a Washington-based attorney and writer specialising in privacy, freedom of information and communications issues. He is Deputy Director of Privacy International and a Senior Fellow at the Electronic Privacy Information Centre

YAMAN AKDENIZ

Anonymous now

Surfing through cyberspace leaves a trail of clues to your identity. Online privacy can be had but it doesn't come easy

Anonymity is essential to democracy and has been a vital tool for the preservation of political speech and discourse throughout history. As a concept it is closely related to free speech and to privacy. The Internet boom in the 1990s created new opportunities for communications and for discussion. Internet technology allows genuinely anonymous communication, and this can be used for many purposes; socially useful, but also criminal.

Political activists, human rights organisations and dissident movements in repressive regimes increasingly rely on anonymous email to publicise human rights abuses in their countries. Furthermore, users can engage in anonymous whistle-blowing, receive counselling or join in all forms of discussions.

There are many global organisations dealing with human rights abuses, such as Human Rights Watch and Amnesty International, who use the Internet to communicate with their members or with dissident groups. Before governments can suppress the dissemination of critical writings and reports, the authors can distribute their work outside repressive regimes. It is well known that Burmese dissidents and the Mexican Zapatistas use the Internet to communicate with the rest of the world – this isn't incidental to their work, it's a key aspect of their strategy. Anonymity and the use of strong encryption tools can help to preserve and expand political discourse and the dissemination of information related to human rights abuses.

Cryptography and anonymity are essential and powerful tools. Cryptographic techniques not only conceal information, they can also authenticate it. For example, recipients of electronic alerts, such as those sent by Amnesty International, the American Civil Liberties Union

(ACLU) and the Tibetan Government in Exile, can ensure that the alerts have not been altered by those wishing to disrupt the group's activities. Users of the Critical Path AIDS Project's website, of Stop Prisoner Rape ('SPR') in the USA and of the Samaritans in Britian rely on anonymity. Many members of SPR's mailing list would not be involved were it not for guaranteed anonymity, such is the stigma of prisoner rape. It is vital that this kind of user can gain access to information while remaining anonymous, and it should be their right to do so in this context.

Internet privacy activists have developed anonymous re-mailer programs that address these concerns. An anonymous re-mailer is simply a computer service that forwards emails to other addresses over the Internet. But the re-mailer also strips off the 'header' from the messages, which shows where they came from and who sent them. The most untraceable re-mailers use public key cryptography which allows unprecedented anonymity both to groups who wish to communicate in complete privacy and to whistle-blowers who have reason to fear persecution.

According to Patrick Ball of the science and human rights programme at the American Association for the Advancement of Science: 'When messages are resent from a truly anonymous re-mailer, the header information is set either to a deliberately misleading address, or to randomly generated characters. There is no record of the connection between the sending address and the destination address. For greater security, many users program messages to pass through five to 20 re-mailers before the message arrives at its final destination. This technique, known as chaining, assures greater security than sending through a single re-mailer. Even if some re-mailers keep secret records of their transactions, a single honest re-mailing system will protect the user. One disadvantage is that unless the sender has identified herself in the body of the message, the recipient has no way to reply to an anonymously sent message' (*ACLU v Miller,* 1997).

One of the best-known anonymous re-mailers on the Internet, *anon.penet.fi,* was offered for more than three years by Johann Helsingius. Among its users were Amnesty International, the Samaritans and Britain's West Mercia Police who used *anon.penet.fi* as part of their 'Crimestoppers' anonymous informing scheme.

In *Mrs. McIntyre in Cyberspace: Some thoughts on anonymity,* Jonathan Wallace writes: 'I may have a good idea you will not consider if you

72

9 70334 876044

Cooper

know my name. Or I may individually fear retaliation if my identity is revealed. Anonymity is therefore good, because it encourages greater diversity of speech.' A good example of this is *Anonymizer.com*, an online project founded by Lance Cottrell, author of the world's most secure anonymous re-mailer, Mixmaster. Anonymizer offers a forum for anonymous discussions and also provides anonymous Web surfing. Anonymizer's Kosovo project allowed individuals to report on conditions and human rights violations from within the war zone, without fear of government retaliation.

Online anonymity is therefore important both to free speech and privacy just as anonymity and anonymous publishing have been for thousands of years in the offline world. It is essential for participation in online equivalents of Alcoholics Anonymous and similar groups. Individuals have a desire and a right to this kind of privacy that should not be abridged for the pursuit of vaguely defined infractions.

Yet this is precisely the plan of governments and law enforcement agencies worldwide. US Attorney General Janet Reno said earlier this year: 'While the Internet and other information technologies are bringing enormous benefits to society, they also provide new opportunities for criminal behaviour.' Although anonymity has important benefits for human rights, law enforcement bodies and the media generally link anonymity with cyber-crimes, or claim that anonymity would allow criminals to use the Internet without the possibility of detection. Such well-publicised fears include anonymous communications for hate mail, child pornography and fraud. A White House report, '*The Electronic Frontier: The Challenge of Unlawful Conduct Involving the Use of the Internet*', published in March found that: 'Individuals who wish to use a computer as a tool to facilitate unlawful activity may find that the Internet provides a vast, inexpensive, and potentially anonymous way to commit unlawful acts, such as fraud, the sale or distribution of child pornography, the sale of guns or drugs or other regulated substances without regulatory protections and the unlawful distribution of computer software or other creative material protected by intellectual property rights.' Elsewhere, the report claims: 'Law enforcement agencies are faced with the need to evaluate and to determine the source, typically on very short notice, of anonymous e-mails that contain bomb threats against a given building or threats to cause serious bodily injury.'

Although the report recognises the desire for anonymity for the legitimate needs described above, it describes anonymous email accounts as 'the proverbial double-edged sword ... such services can plainly frustrate legitimate law enforcement efforts'. The report concludes: 'Internet-based activities should be treated consistently with physical world activities and in a technology-neutral way to further important societal goals ... National policies concerning anonymity and accountability on the Internet thus need to be developed in a way that takes account of privacy, authentication, and public safety concerns.'

However, it is not at all clear how the US government plans to address law enforcement needs while preserving the rights of individual Internet users. In the past, there have been attempts in the US to pass legislation that would bar anonymous communications. In 1997, the ACLU challenged a Georgia law on the grounds that it restricted free speech. ACLU and others stated that the Georgia law was unconstitutionally vague and overbroad because it barred online users from using pseudonyms or communicating anonymously over the Internet.

The ACLU responded to the latest White House report by stating: 'Anonymity on the Internet is not a thorny issue; it is a constitutional right. The United States Supreme Court held that the constitution grants citizens the right to speak anonymously.' Moreover, the ACLU also warned that 'an end to Internet anonymity would chill free expression in cyberspace and strip away one of the key structural privacy protections enjoyed by Internet users.'

Those who call for the prohibition of anonymous re-mailers or other restrictions on anonymity fail to recognise the potential damage to freedom of expression online. The European Convention on Human Rights recognises freedom of expression as a right and also recognises the circumstances in which it may be legitimately suppressed: 'Everyone has the right to freedom of expression. This right should include freedom to hold opinions and to receive and impart information and ideas without interference by public authority and regardless of frontiers ... The exercise of these freedoms, since it carries with it duties and responsibilities, may be subject to such formalities, conditions, restrictions or penalties as are prescribed by law and are necessary in a democratic society, in the interests of national security ... for the prevention of disorder or crime ... for the protection of the reputation or rights of others.'

The importance of anonymity as a facilitator of free speech has been affirmed by the European Court of Human Rights (*Goodwin v UK,* 1996). The Court recognised that the press has a vital watchdog role in a healthy democratic society and that this function could be undermined if journalists are not allowed to keep the sources of their information confidential. In this case, the Court concluded that the application of the law of contempt to a recalcitrant journalist was not necessary where the subject of the damaging story had already obtained an injunction against publication. It is not clear that the same level of protection would be afforded by the European Court to the idle gossip of non-press speakers, but anonymous 'political speech' would certainly deserve protection.

Moreover, there may also be instances where Internet postings may lead to persecution if the identity of the individual is known. The Supreme Court in *NAACP v Alabama ex rel Patterson,* 1958) stated: 'Inviolability of privacy in group association may in many circumstances be indispensable to preservation of freedom of association.'

Apart from facilitating freedom of expression, anonymity also enables users to prevent surveillance and monitoring of their activities on the Internet. Total anonymity may be possible by the use of such privacy enhancing technologies as 'Freedom: Absolute Privacy Protection', (*www.freedom.net*), which works seamlessly alongside Internet browsers and other applications. This useful piece of software gives total protection of an individual's personal information and personal security.

Whether the importance of anonymity on the Internet will be recognised by future regulatory initiatives remains to be seen. Right now it is legislation that threatens online privacy and technology that protects it. Privacy software tools and services are multiplying; you can be as private as you want to be, just be careful where you click. ❏

Yaman Akdeniz *is the director of Cyber-Rights & Cyber-Liberties (UK),* www.cyber-rights.org, *and is the author of* Sex on the Net? The Dilemma of Policing Cyberspace (*Reading: South Street Press, 1999*)

Libraries & Culture

EDITOR: Donald G. Davis, Jr., University of Texas at Austin

Libraries & Culture is an interdisciplinary journal that explores the significance of collections of recorded knowledge — their creation, organization, preservation, and utilization — in the context of cultural and social history, unlimited as to time and place. Many articles deal with North American topics, but **L & C** also publishes articles on library history in other countries, as well as topics dealing with ancient and medieval libraries.

"Topics are diverse...Book reviews are detailed, evaluative, and scholarly in approach. This is a delightful journal, beautifully illustrated."
— **Magazines for Libraries 1995**

RECENT CONTENTS FOR 2000

Single copy rates: Individual $14, Institution $22,
Canada/Mexico, add $2.50; other foreign, add $5 (airmail).
Yearly subscription rates: Individual $30, Institution $59,
Student/Retired $18,
Canada/Mexico, add $10; other foreign, add $20 (airmail).
Refunds available only on unshipped quantities of current subscriptions.

University of Texas Press Journals
Box 7819, Austin, Texas 78713-7819
Phone # 512-471-4531, Fax # 512-320-0668, journals@uts.cc.utexas.edu

DAVID BURKE

The spy in the corner

Orwell's ultimate invasion of personal privacy, the telescreen, is an also-ran next to digital TV. It's high definition, widescreen and it even watches your kids

Never before has so much entertaining technology been offered to, or aimed at, people in every intimate part of their lives. We are in need of a scale by which to measure each new machine's respect for our humanity. Stuck into the ground at one end of any such measure would be those devices designed from the beginning to observe and manipulate people from a distance, automatically, without their knowledge or consent. Such extreme examples help darken the lines between systems we use and those that use us.

Digital interactive television was offered as a blank page on which marketers, public relations consultants and social engineers of all kinds could build their dream machine. The result is a real-time, two-way pipe in and out of people's living rooms, built to record and analyse every click they make on their remotes. On average, people watch TV for four hours a day; so half the time they are not working or sleeping, they will spend under observation.

'Somehow they feel they're sitting there – it's just them and their TV,' says Matthew Timms of Two Way TV in London, 'even though the reality is it's got a wire going straight back to someone's computer.'

The new technology is impressive. The huge amount of data generated will be linked to existing demographic and household databanks. It will run past artificial intelligence software, capable of learning and adapting to individual behaviours.

What's old is the business model. Like ordinary TV, and unlike the Internet – for now at least – digital interactive TV will be run by a few corporations and governments. As with ordinary television, the entry costs are enormous and the real products are the viewers, captured for persuasion. As marketing consultant Pat Dade says of his work: 'We're all just trying to change or reinforce existing behaviour.'

While systems from Sky, NTL, Telewest, Microsoft and soon AOL are sold to the public with words like 'control' and 'empowerment', Dade describes in excited terms the power and control *he* and others like him will soon have. Their use of psychology, data warehousing and neutral network software, raise a number of broader social and political issues that demand attention.

The first is the unprecedented targeting of children. 'Target' is a provocative word, but is justified in all its meanings when marketers and broadcasters attend conferences with names like 'Kid Power 99', and lectures such as 'Marketing to Young Kids by Targeting the Gatekeeper'; 'Parents, Nagging Kids and Purchase decisions'.

Such ambitious attempts to infiltrate and control families show that marketing has changed fundamentally, from mass announcement to individual engagement. This new approach is called 'one-to-one marketing' or 'relationship marketing'. It's the great hope of advertisers and broadcasters at a time when markets and audiences are fragmenting or learning to avoid ordinary commercials. The idea is to focus not on products but on lifelong relationships with customers, who can then be persuaded to form strong brand or provider loyalties.

One-to-one requires a 'learning relationship' in which sellers must obtain everything they can about a consumers' needs and interests, and interactive television was created to do the gathering.

'It's about creating as much information about each consumer as you possibly can,' says Mark Albert of Alto, a database consultancy now working with interactive broadcasters, 'and using that in the most expedient manner to get your product to them, and them using your product in specific consumer segments, ideally the segment of one.'

Raw data from every television will be used for geo-demographic, lifestyle, market segment and even psychographic modelling. Over time, artificial intelligence will pick out digital fingerprints that link viewers to other people who have similar emotional needs.

And the viewers with the simplest needs, and the least resistance to long-term persuasion, are children. Pat Dade was hoping to work with video game producer Electronic Arts to produce a game capable of assessing players according to Abraham Maslov's hierarchy of needs: 'We know that when we're playing games, we're actually being more of what we are on the inside. Remember it's the kids who are growing up that we're talking about, who see the Internet as a friendly, dialoguey kind of thing.'

But when the young programmers at Electronic Arts were shown the specification, they refused to work on the project. Dade should have gone to Scott Randall at BrandGames in New York, who told an audience at Kid Power 99: 'There's never been a reliable way to turn media "impressions" into one-to-one relationships, or to service those relationships with continuity and consistency.'

Until now. Randall went on to describe his company's CDs, Internet and interactive TV games that befriend young players and service their relationships – not with other children or adults, or even salesmen – but with walking, talking, laughing, playing brands. He describes a multimedia game his company created for General Mills in which a child's favourite baseball team can take on various cartoon characters from the box fronts of the company's cereals: 'Well, the kid sits around playing this for 40 trillion hours and goes to the store. He's just spent 30 zillion hours with these nine characters. They're his friends. "Ohhh, there's the guy, aw, Mommy, here's my friend the Trix rabbit"!'

Identification with brands, either as animated friends or as oneself, is the new experience that interactive television will offer children all over the world, for hours every day. 'Character consultants' can now be hired to help companies develop animated animals or action figures that speak to children's emotional needs. What the characters then say to those needs is, of course, up to the company.

Microsoft and Mattel spent US$40 million developing Actimates Barney, a talking, singing purple dinosaur that takes instructions from signals beamed out with the Barney TV programme. While similar technology running a Pokémon doll claims to 'set kids imaginations free', the Actimates website more accurately describes Barney as 'a viewing buddy' that 'helps kids get more involved with the programme'.

At a conference on the subject in Pittsburgh, BJ Fogg of Stanford's Persuasive Technology Laboratory warned of a time when such a doll could sense that a sponsor's fast-food restaurant was nearby and chirp, 'Hmm … I smell french fries. I'm hungry, aren't you?'

Gathering information and creating profiles of viewers is only half the equation. What really excites the people who make interactive television is the way it creates experimental conditions in the home. Your television will be able to show you something, monitor how you respond, and then show you something else, based on what you did. Here, Mark Albert of Alto speaks the new language of home entertainment: 'You have to create some control group testing, in effect throw people some placebos. So if we're trying to increase their spend, or increase their usage or increase their customer satisfaction scores, we'll take one group and split it down the middle and expose it to two separate batches of data presentation.'

And again, this cycle of stimulus, measurement and response will be run by artificial intelligence software. Your television can just keep trying things on you for years, until it gets the behaviour it has been told to look for. This loop of experimentation is where we may live very soon. If you think about it, digital interactive television has been designed to work like a caring parent. That is what makes it so frightening. That's 'targeting' taken to its logical conclusion.

A further concern is that data protection laws could soon be useless.

European law requires companies to register how they gather and use personal information. Citizens must be given access to the data held about them and some say over who else can read it. The US has no data protection legislation, but just this year passed a law requiring parental permission before a child could surrender personal information over the Internet. How long will such statutes mean anything?

Once I have a thinking, learning, adapting machine in my house, able to monitor my behaviour and respond by its control of everything I see or hear for four hours every day, then 'personal information' is just some machine code, or a set of most effective parameters. None of it need ever leave my house, because the very people who would gather it are now living with me. ❏

David Burke *is the author of* Spy TV *(Slab-o-Concrete, 1999). Additional research by Deirdre Devers. More at* www.spyinteractive.com

GREG PALAST

Kissing the whip

Britain's government is the most secretive in the developed world, maintaining its private sphere with a myriad forms of gagging legislation, overt, subtle and crude. Nor are journalists always eager to leap to the defence of their peers

On 17 March, on an order from the London Metropolitan Police, reporter Martin Bright of the *Observer*, his editor and lawyers for the editor of its weekday sister paper, the *Guardian*, were brought before a judge at the Old Bailey. On pain of imprisonment and unlimited fines, the British court ordered the reporter and editors to turn over all internal notes relating to stories about a former MI5 agent. The reporter and the editors refused.

One week later at a black-tie soirée at the Hilton Hotel, I found myself in a meandering, champagne-lubricated debate with a disturbingly articulate gent defending the government's right to censor and restrict news reports. My interlocutor, *Guardian* editor and *Observer* CEO Alan Rusbridger, was the very man facing time in the Queen's dungeon for refusing the court order.

I was not surprised. It is the subtle brilliance of British censorship and news suppression that its prime victims, the nation's editors and reporters, have developed a nodding acceptance of the principles justifying limits on their freedom, a curious custom of English journalists to kiss the whip that lashes them.

Rusbridger challenged me: 'You wouldn't want a [news] photographer taking pictures of your family over your garden fence, would you?' Well, no. The death of Princess Diana – in the public's mind, a victim of invasive press hounds, has turned a concern for protecting privacy into a treacherous obsession. Under this banner of respecting privacy, Prime Minister Tony Blair's government obtained a block on publication of his children's nanny's diaries. The convenient tool of privacy was also the cloak used to conceal ministers' salaries, education statistics and even the records of a 'private' conversation on a phone from Downing Street in which a Blair adviser privately sold access to government officials. Accepting a zone of privacy around government has become the first, attractive step down that slippery slope to journalists' accepting state censorship (*Index* 5/98, 2/95).

The news community's response to the writs against Rusbridger, Bright and their papers was slow to form. In a land of cautious protest and measured defence, the *Observer* itself delayed for a week covering its own punishment, unsure whether readers found their paper's repression newsworthy.

Weeks passed. Finally, a petition was got up, signed by media notables. With their plea to the government to drop the prosecutions, the petitioners conceded: 'We recognise the need to protect national security,' a mannered diffidence to the state's ultimate authority over the printed word grating to my American ears. The journalists also demanded: 'The Official Secrets Act should be reformed to allow a public interest defence.' *Reformed?* The Official Secrets Act prohibits the publication of almost any document or fact which the government chooses to conceal. The polite protesters would grant the right of the Crown to arrest journalists, but they requested wide exceptions. Petition organisers knew a demand to abolish the repressive Act outright would have chased away key signatories.

The *Guardian* editorialised in its own defence, but again, its complaint was carefully circumscribed. The paper targeted the plain silliness of the government's writ. The *Guardian* had done nothing more than print a former MI5 agent's letter to the editor. Ironically, the former agent, David Shayler, grumbled in his letter that the *Guardian* did not take his allegations against the government seriously. The government demanded the newspaper hand over the physical copy of the agent's letter (as it turned out, the computer tape holding an email message) despite the fact that Shayler himself sent a copy of the letter directly to the authorities.

Similarly, the *Observer* report contained little more than a note that a US Internet site had posted information corroborating Shayler's accusations. Apparently, Shayler had tipped off the *Observer* to this public information. While *any* communication by an ex-agent violates the Official Secrets Act, the police did not need the reporter's letter files as unique evidence of Shayler's alleged violation of the law: Shayler himself had sent the government copies of his messages to the paper.

Yet, the sheer foolishness of the government's demanding documents already in its possession is evidence of a more sinister aim. By showing it will punish minor infractions of its secrecy laws, the government succeeds in freezing any journalist's attempt to dig out deeper and more dangerous truths concealed within secretive agencies. Worse, journalists, defending their minor infractions, trap themselves into justifying the greater censorship. 'As a newspaper,' wrote the *Observer*, 'we have no difficulty with secrets or with the principle that secrecy, where necessary, should be protected by the law.'

By agreeing to limit themselves to 'legitimate' inquiries, to use the timid terminology of the journalists' petition, the papers open the door to state policing to root out the 'illegitimate'.

Most US readers, who still think of Britain as mother of our democracy, will be surprised to learn that the United Kingdom remains one of the hemisphere's only nations without a written constitutional guarantee of free speech and press. That is about to change in October as Article 10 of the European Convention on Human Rights becomes British law. The Convention will allow Britons, for the first time, 'to receive and impart information and ideas without interference by public authority'. The case against the *Guardian* and the *Observer* is the government's pre-emptive strike to define away those new rights.

The court and government were quick to agree that the new Human Rights law applied to the current prosecution of reporter Bright and the newspapers. This was not good news. Whereas the US constitution states: 'Congress shall not restrict the freedom of the press nor of speech', no ifs, ands or buts, the European Convention adds a nasty little codicil, 'Part 2'.

In the 17 March hearing, the judge ruled that the right to 'receive and impart information' was subject to Part 2's 'restrictions and penalties in the interests of national security.'

On 15 April, the censorship-self-censorship vaudeville opened a new act. That day, Bright saw a copy of a four-year-old MI5 document detailing the security agency's bungled attempt to recruit a Libyan spy, a cock-up which appears to have led to the murder of a Libyan dissident living in London. The 'TOP SECRET DELICATE SOURCE UK

THE SECURITY SERVICE

G9A|5

TEL: 0171-828 8688 Ext 88300
GTN: 3033
FAX: 0171-630 1428

Our Ref: PF690551/G9/0

Date: 1 December 1995

Dear ▆▆,

Libyan Intelligence Service activity in the UK

31. ▆▆▆ELYA is the focal point for Libyan intelligence activity in the UK and is becoming increasingly active in his own right. His continued presence in the UK can only serve to facilitate further intelligence activity.

32. ▆▆▆ELYA's expulsion would severely disrupt the Libyan intelligence effort in the UK. It would also send a strong message to the Libyan regime that HMG will not tolerate Libyan intelligence activity on British soil.

EYES' document can be read by anyone with a mouse and time on their hands at *www.cryptome.org*. Bright drafted a story (with Antony Barnett) about the information on the website.

Despite its open publication on the site, repeating this information invited criminal and civil penalties. (In fact, *reading* the website's content is a crime in Britain) To avoid another writ, the *Observer* contacted the Defence Advisory Committee, the 'D-Notice' committee, a kind of government confessional where journalists may whisper their unpublished thoughts and information and ask, in confidence: 'If we publish, will we have sinned against the state?' The agency suggested that if the paper could prove its news report contained no new news – an interesting restriction – then prosecution *might* not follow.

However, there was another censor yet to contact: the Treasury

Solicitor holds a permanent injunction, granted two years ago against any British newspaper publishing any information whatsoever from former agents. Just five minutes before the print deadline, the Treasury telephoned. Four hours passed (and four editions with front-page filler where the article could have run) as the government bargained with the editors and the paper's lawyers who, in the face of ruinous fines, found themselves with little choice but to fax to MI5 the draft of the story.

The paper asked two simple questions: Would publication violate the law? And, can we publish? The government said it would not stop publication, but neither would it promise not to prosecute the reporters and editor if publication went ahead. MI5's position had a serpentine brilliance: blocking the article would get them an 'OBSERVER GAGGED AGAIN!' headline. By keeping open the *hint* – but not the *threat* – of prosecution, the official spooks meant to lure the paper into spiking the story while the government could claim it censored nothing.

The paper finally published in its last edition, though it 'voluntarily' left off the website's address. Bright finds the procedure deadly to the ethics of news coverage. 'It's crazy but the law says we can't do what journalists should always do: check with the sources, review the key documents. We have to break the law to break the news.'

The D-Notice Committee, the reluctance to ban publication outright, the seemingly sympathetic bargaining, all serve to foster the habit of self-censorship. Rarely does government brandish the implements of coercion because news people are bred to a strong sense of the boundaries of public discourse. In this class-poisoned society, elite reporters and editors are lured by the thrill of joining the inner circle of ministers and titled military intelligence men. The cost of admission is gentlemanly circumspection.

Britons, as they constantly remind me, are subjects not citizens. British-born journalist Christopher Hitchens, scourge of authorities on two continents, stunned Americans by submitting to deposition by US government prosecutors during the impeachment trial of President Bill Clinton. Clearly, habits of subjugation die hard. ❏

American journalist **Greg Palast**, *based in New York and London, writes for the* Observer. *He is best known as the reporter whose undercover work led to 'Lobbygate,' the first exposé of corruption within the Blair government*

THIRD WORLD QUARTERLY
Journal of Emerging Areas

Editor: **Shahid Qadir,** *Royal Holloway, University of London, UK*

SUPPORTED BY AN INTERNATIONAL EDITORIAL BOARD

Third World Quarterly (TWQ) is the leading journal of scholarship and policy in the field of international studies. For more than two decades, it has set the agenda on development discourses of the global debate. As the most influential academic journal covering the emerging worlds, *TWQ* is at the forefront of analysis and commentary on fundamental issues of global concern.

Third World Quarterly examines all the issues that affect the many Third Worlds as we enter the threshold of the Third Millennium. *TWQ* is not averse to publishing provocative and exploratory articles, especially if they have the merit of opening up emerging areas of research that have not been given sufficient attention.

Third World Quarterly is a journal that looks beyond strict "development studies", providing an alternative and over-arching reflective analysis of micro-economic and grassroot efforts of development practitioners and planners. It furnishes expert and interdisciplinary insight into crucial issues before they impinge upon media attention, as well as coverage of the very latest publications in its comprehensive book review section.

Third World Quarterly acts as an almanac linking the academic terrains of the various contemporary area studies – African, Asian, Latin American and Middle Eastern – in an interdisciplinary manner with the publication of informative, innovative and investigative articles. Contributions are rigorously assessed by regional experts.

Subscription rates *Volume 21, 2000, 6 issues. ISSN 0143-6597*

Institutional rate: *US$498   £298*
Personal rate: *US$108   £66*

For further information or to request a sample copy please contact:

Carfax Publishing, Taylor & Francis Ltd, Customer Services Department, Rankine Road, Basingstoke, Hants RG24 8PR, UK

Tel: +44 (0)1256 813000 *Fax:* +44 (0)1256 330245
E-mail: enquiry@tandf.co.uk *WWW:* http://www.tandf.co.uk/journals

BRUCE STERLING

The worst may already have happened

The tenth annual 'Computers, Freedom and Privacy' conference took place in April 2000. Hurray for the brave little world of electronic civil liberties.

People have grown used to computer networks, and have assimilated and domesticated them to a truly remarkable degree. It's hard to recall now how utopian and abstract this was a mere decade ago. The Internet is omnipresent in the year 2000, about as futuristic and astounding as running water.

But technology marches, while the law crawls. As the girders and curtain walls of cyberspace fly up, there's a bland public expectation that high-tech developments will somehow work out for the best – while the legal and political foundation is mere rubble.

Maybe we'll just have to live that way: suspended in mid-air. Legal professor Lawrence Lessig, in his recent book *Code and Other Laws of Cyberspace* (Basic Books, 1999), suggests a new paradigm for befuddled legislators: henceforth, software should be seen as the 'law' of computers. 'Code is law.' Professor Lessig argues that merely legal attempts to regulate computer use are doomed to irrelevance. Today's enlightened Solon upgrades himself, to become a kind of constitutional interface designer.

This is a very interesting development, a strain of political thinking quite new in the world. Basically, it's the 'embrace and extend' Microsoft philosophy, carried into governance. If you can't beat em, become em. Democratic statesmen (deftly avoiding the danger of utter irrelevance) make wise cyber-design decisions that protect the citizenry.

'Protect them from what?' the neophyte may ask. 'Terrorists, child pornographers, drug dealers and the mafia' – ten years ago, those were the standard, notorious 'Four Horsemen of the Infocalypse.' Lessig is more experienced than this, and more advanced in his thinking. Apparently, he basically wants to protect us from Microsoft. Or at least, from some looming menace of an unregulatable, profit-driven, cruelly-invasive net.

Lessig's vision cross-breeds Washington's sage oversight with Silicon Valley's rapid development and just-in-time shipping. My good 'code' outdoes your wicked 'code' because the US government smiles upon it, giving it some critical early edge in the technological adoption curves. Once wise standards are firmly set in place, technological lock-in occurs, and certain frowned-upon actions need no longer even be outlawed, because they've been rendered impossible.

To give it its due, this is a practical, hands-on and very contemporary vision, but there is little comfort to be gained there for traditional fans of 'freedom and privacy'. Freedom and privacy are supposed to be basic human rights, not browser plug-ins. Still, given the evident trends, what else is government activism to do? National legislators (archaically based in their merely-territorial sovereignty) are basically impotent to shape the global flight of data. They're in very much the same basket as contemporary labour unions, impotent to shape the global flight of capital.

Mind you, people, us citizens, can still be effectively apprehended, arrested and jailed by governments (nowhere with more gusto than in the world's leading Internet pioneer, the United States). But data moves even faster and more randomly than money does.

To shift the argument from mere democracy to the giddy heights of software design: national governments can't out-design the market. Governments don't have the personnel, the talent, or the consumer credibility. Consider the grim death-by-inches of France's Minitel. Consider the even more miserable doom of the US government designed-and-approved 'Clipper Chip'. The Clipper Chip was a means of purported 'privacy protection' that served the interests of the FBI first, industry second and private individuals as a remote third. Designed by government agents, it was, of course, about basic government interests. The Clipper Chip was promptly rejected in the market, worldwide, instantly, not merely with indifference, but with virulent contempt.

To imagine the US government cookin' up some red-hot Web code is just not very likely; it's about as plausible as the Supreme Court recording a three-minute hit pop single.

The Internet's code was created mostly by academics. It comes in publicly accessible chunks, and drifts in and out of the scattered hands of an interactive gaggle of hobbyists. Arrest one of them for some ingenious flouting of the public good (blithely cracking DeCSS code, for instance), and he'll merely point at someone else in distant Norway.

These technicians can't be held accountable. Unlike doctors, lawyers, and engineers, programmers don't have licences or review boards. Furthermore, though they may design and strew clever software tools all over the landscape with joyful abandon, programmers don't control the actions of the Internet's end-users. Appeals to their civic spirit won't help much, since software programmers have very little unanimity in their motives or intentions. To have ten of them in a room is to have 15 feuds.

'The architectural is political', in the words of Mitch Kapor. The political architecture of the Internet is decentralised, anarchic, post-national, extremely fast-moving and rather slipshod. The realm's tattered pretence at law and order is accordingly dominated by good-old-boyism, scandal-mongering and moral panic. Especially, moral panic. Moral panic is its signature political motif.

Moral panic haunts cyberspace for a very good reason. There is very little else that can make any difference. If you cannot make a firm legal argument and compel any serious attention; if you lack any physical ability to control and corral the actors; if you can't buy them off; and if you can't even build the thing properly, then, finally, provoking a panic is a tactic of genuine promise. Better to light a brushfire, and perhaps provoke some useful mass stampede, than to declare oneself entirely irrelevant to the course of events.

So the Internet's geek technicians carry out their potent activities in relative peace and obscurity. What passes for Internet government and politics is all fads, hype, plagues, scandals, sudden jolts and muffled, distant hammering. Computer-activism of all ideologies is routinely dominated by terrifying worst-case scenarios, as small groups of zealots scream imprecations, blow high-tech smoke and wave a wide variety of bloody shirts.

Internet pundits routinely employ fantastic, dizzying prose in even minor matters. For years on end, the political rhetoric of cyberspace has been chock-full of monstrous phantoms, deployed like glossy *Star Wars* trading cards: nuclear terrorists, mass corporate enslavement, hacker infowar, Orwellian computer regimes.

And then there's privacy. 'Privacy' is a sound political issue, but it's not very market-friendly. Certain gizmos for enhancing data privacy are commercially available, but they've never been mass-market major consumer items, so they don't compel much sustained investment. Internet activism tends to follow cyber-industrial development. Privacy lacks IPOs, stock booms and commercial glitz, the lifeblood of the modern Internet. Internet privacy has therefore been forced into a secondary niche compared with, say, potentially lucrative fair-access issues. People can raise millions to digitally wire the homes of the poor. No one will pay to leave the poor unwired and undisturbed – even though anybody's privacy is profoundly enhanced when their home is free of a direct connection to thousands of Internet databanks.

Privacy simply isn't very profitable. Privacy is, however, a first-class source of moral panic. Once a digital-privacy scandal manages to take root and spread, the effects are as sudden and devastating as a computer virus, as unsuspecting entities like Lotus and DoubleClick have learned to their cost.

There is scarcely a better method to get under someone's skin than to suggest that they are being watched. 'The guilty flee when no man pursueth.' We all feel guilty when observed against our will, for there are innate contradictions of private behaviour and public life that can never be successfully reconciled. We do many worthy, healthy, life-affirming things in privacy that would earn us lifelong humiliation if publicised. Consider our normal behaviour in bathrooms and bedrooms. There are reservoirs of primal Freudian panic here that can never be soothed.

The contemporary world excels, however, at making the invisible visible. Our brains can be CAT-scanned and the planet Venus mapped through radar. Why should some mere closed door shield us from prying eyes? The physical limits to the creation and flow of media are in abject collapse. 'Surveillance' is a pejorative term, but 'surveillance' is media. They are the same thing. Better 'media', better 'surveillance'. Our 'data shadows' (a lovely, very telling coinage from the digital privacy community) spread from us in scary, surreptitious, unsuspected ways.

Security videocams are tiny nowadays: they go unnoticed and unresented. Our telephone bills can finger our friends and relations for the delight of investigators. Credit-card transactions paint our daily economic activities for the grim attention of Big Brother (or, far more likely, the profit of 'Big Broker'). Our online purchases are instantly catalogued, sorted and data-mined. Medical records detail our pain and weakness. Scary, Frankenstein-style genetic scans suddenly abound, so we find ourselves leaving unsuspected trails of our own shed DNA; we can be smelled back to our very lairs by anyone with a sequencer and a cotton swab.

Then there's the mighty power of the digitised state, with its passports, checkpoints, licence bureaus, tax records, police wiretaps, and its national data-banks of dissidents, aliens and criminals (if indeed one's state even bothers to make those fine distinctions). The oldest, ablest and best-financed foes of privacy are entities that are huge, wealthy, well-equipped, unspeakable, untraceable and publicly unaccountable. They are 'spooks,' the espionage services. That's certainly a lasting boon for paranoiacs.

How do we depart from speculation and scaremongering, to get some sense of what this means for the daily lives of human beings?

It's good to grasp what's technically possible: but mere possibility is very far from likelihood. Engineers are never good social theorists. An increase in our technical capacity certainly doesn't make us any more dispassionate or scientific. The near-bacterial outbreak of computers in our homes and offices hasn't made people one whit more computerlike. On the contrary: greater technical power, like any form of greater power, magnifies our hidden eccentricities.

Consider, for instance, indecent exposure. This minor crime is a particularly squalid rupture of privacy. It's an unsettling shock for the victim, and a lifelong humiliation for the perpetrator, should he be identified and apprehended.

Now imagine that massively magnified, blown up by a factor of millions. Imagine being publicly transformed into a sexual pervert, quite against one's own will and intention, as part and parcel of a vast, lubricious, septic, media orgy, on millions of screens around the world. That is the kind of heroic agony that only the iron will of a Bill Clinton can endure.

This is precisely what an out-of-control collapse in privacy can look like in real life. Incredible, ludicrous, bizarre. Office gossip, a dalliance, recorded phone calls, websites, lawyers and cable TV, leading, step after outlandish step, into a full-scale constitutional *coup d'état*. Big, yes, squalid, yes; but never recognised and dealt with as an issue of privacy.

This episode was by no means without harbingers. In 1987, when

Judge Robert Bork was nominated for the US Supreme Court, enterprising enemies discovered and revealed the records of his videotape rentals. Bork's enemies were, of course, fishing through the records for pornography. Had they found any smut in Bork's rental records, the Judge's nomination would have become an instant debacle, probably rivalling the bizarre sexual circus of Judge Clarence Thomas, some years later. Judge Bork, to the disappointment of his persecutors, had no fondness for video pornography. However, such was the existential horror of Congress at this attempted porn-smear that they successfully passed one of the few American privacy initiatives of the last 20 years, the Video Privacy Protection Act of 1988.

This rare triumph of focused legislation made US 'videotape service providers' liable for civil actions if they revealed their rental records. But this Act was a stopgap at best. In an age of freely available, booming Internet pornography, the sticky fluidity of sexual data is not to be restrained by mere congressmen. By ten years later, 1998, the communications revolution had advanced so marvellously that Congress itself deliberately piped highly salacious details about oral sex over the Internet. Same impulses. Same motives. Far better technology.

The president's impeachment was not some panicky worst-case scenario. Nobody could have made this up. No mere computer-pundit could have predicted or even imagined this. This was real life. This historically unprecedented invasion of the presidential genitalia was never recognised as a technological violation of expected social norms.

No such connection was made, no particular worthy lesson learned, and no law was passed. Instead, the American government was simply wrecked and stricken, as if by voodoo. All of the major figures in the drama, seemingly enchanted, were plunged week by week, month by month, into Stygian depths of utter prurience. Historians should marvel.

It should be clear that mere indiscretion had very little to do with this spectacular course of events. Indeed, the president's foremost political enemy, the Republican Speaker of the House, was carrying out a far more reckless and indiscreet extramarital affair of his own, even as his subordinates plotted the president's downfall. Believe it or not, politicians somewhere are having illicit sex even as I type these words. The notion that politicians, who are affable, charismatic and persuasive by nature, will abjure future acts of seduction is absurd. Sex is a given. It's the jet-propulsion of private acts onto the public stage that has warped the status quo.

Worse yet, no mere law can be passed that can physically protect future chief executives from novel forms of surveillance. To assert control, one would have to pursue a vast array of audiovisual and recording technology, Lawrence Lessig-style, and somehow guide its engineering and design.

If 'code is law' on the Internet, then the clearest intent of that code is to move any kind of data, anywhere, any time, any place. Once data is weightlessly blown in instants across dozens of national borders to thousands of users, it cannot be successfully recalled or expunged, by anyone, or any agency, or any law, anywhere.

Given these technical realities, the resultant, unthinkably-humiliating squalor can only be boldly and resolutely faced down – as indeed the uniquely gifted Bill Clinton somehow managed to do.

So, the worst may have already happened. In terms of privacy's political consequence, dethroning the chief executive of the last remaining superpower is about as extreme as political consequence can get. It has happened already; it was truly awful; it's just not understood as 'privacy'.

Computerised loss of privacy needn't be about slow, creeping Orwellisation, where Party doublethink is imposed from on high on the proles. That's a 20th-century model, written back in 1948. Contemporary reality has shifted. Nowadays, it's far more likely to be about repeated, serio-comic, surreal explosions. Farcical bursts of utter weirdness. Fads, hype, plague, scandals, sudden jolts.

The US was probably lucky that this destabilising process surfaced early, and that it failed to destroy the constitution and the presidency. A potential arsenal of sexual espionage is still very much there and ready for use in American politics today, but much like mustard gas, it's been proven to wreak such indiscriminate havoc that it's perhaps a little less likely to be used. Mind you, this is not a merely American ailment. The Russian 'War of Compromats' among Russia's media oligarchs was even more prolonged, debilitating and extreme. The Russian experience probably cost Russia a president. It likely had much to do with the fact that the current Russian president is a career KGB spy.

US politicians uneasily refer to this as the 'politics of personal destruction'. It's not mere malice at work: this would likely be better understood as a politics of high-tech privacy-rupture. The US now combines hugely over-financed campaigns with excellent digital databases. That's a toxic mix. Opposition-research experts haunt every professional campaign, researching and compiling any event in a candidate's life that might be spun as a damaging flaw. The outcome of this rampant digital investigation is not cleaner politics or greater public accountability. Far from it. It's like having one's candidates ritually beaten to death with brooms.

Its a rather bizarre inversion of the grim prognostications of Orwell, who imagined the faceless tyrants in Room 101 picking minor journalists apart. On the contrary, it's those in power who suffer most acutely from dysfunctional privacy policy. To be a British royal has become one of the most hazardous and humiliating jobs in the world.

Maybe we'll just get used to it, and get over it. Or, we might resolve this democratically, if we were able to air the issues fully and frankly, and discuss them in some balanced, constructive way. Unfortunately, the world's true masters of illicit surveillance are very unwilling to let this happen. It's a painful time to be in GCHQ or NSA. The Puzzle Palace, with its acres of Cray supercomputers and legions of mathematicians, is under siege by computerised amateurs. They don't like this, so they take steps behind to impede progress, behind the scenes.

'ECHELON' isn't its real name, but ECHELON is real. The global extent of this hidden colossus beggars public credulity. But ECHELON is not at all futuristic; it's quite old. Cryptography and electronic surveillance were right there at the very cribside when digital computers were born. In a strange moment of Lessig-like rationality, once WWII was over, Winston Churchill brusquely ordered that Alan Turing's code-cracking computers be hammered into chunks and secretly dumped in the North Sea. Politicians knew how to command the field, back in those days.

But the temptations of covert technical power were too strong for democracy to resist. With Truman's secret founding of the National Security Agency, a vast surveillance apparatus was created. Those networks exist, but they are beyond argument, beyond analysis, beyond free debate. Not merely technically obscure, they are deliberately concealed.

This means that democratic legal scholars are mere stalking-horses for democracy's covert spook lords, whose abusive high-tech networks have been covert, unconstitutional and illegal from the beginning. An honest debate about privacy is impossible in these circumstances. The result is a slow shadow-war of geek and spook. The spy networks will remain hidden as long as they're funded. They'll be funded, under the table, as long as there's advantage to be gained from their eavesdropping. Clearly there is some great advantage there. Every embassy has microwave aerials; nobody ever shuts them down. Putin is KGB, while George Bush was CIA. As for perfidious Albion and her official secrets, the less said the better.

When the amazing technical capacities of UK/USA, ECHELON and the Keyhole satellites are revealed, as they surely must be some day, the history of the 20th century will have to be rewritten. Rewritten, decades later if necessary, just as history was rewritten after ENIGMA, Purple Code and Double-Cross.

The odd part is that all this has *already happened* – a loony-libertarian nightmare vision of world-gripping computerised surveillance wasn't just made up by weirdos. It's been puttering along for decades, as real as Volkswagens. Until the microphones and microwave antennas are pulled out of the planet's woodwork and placed on to the negotiating table, no government in the world can be considered an honest broker when it comes to privacy. Least of all the UK/USA, masters of ECHELON and mothers of parliaments. The world's second-oldest profession profits from a double-standard almost as effectively as does its first. ❏

Bruce Sterling is a science-fiction novelist and the author of the non-fiction computer-crime book Hacker Crackdown *(Penguin, 1994)*

INDEX INDEX

Springtime for Serbia

The Milosevic government's repression of the independent media has achieved new heights since January with 20 organisations falling victim to financial reprisals, and ten being summarily suspended or closed under the controversial Public Information Act of October 1998.

Deputy Prime Minister Vojislav Seselj added nationalist vitriol to this piece of scurrilous legal machinery when he told a press conference on 8 February: 'All those who work for the Americans must face the consequences … Be very afraid. You work for a traitorous media.' The vilification was spurred by Seselj's apparent conviction that 'journalists' were accomplices to the assassination one day earlier of defence minister Pavle Bulatovic. He warned journalists they would suffer the same fate.

Print media were the first to feel the backlash. Journalists from weeklies *Glas Javnosti* and *Danas*, the daily *Blic* and Beta news agency were barred from a conference of the Vojvodina Socialist Party on 10 February. A guard explained that only 'eligible' media had been invited. *Blic* and *Glas Javnosti* were 'elegible' for financial countermeasures, however. The commerce ministry quickly ordered that the two papers reduce their cover price for 'making excessive profits'.

On 2 March, it was the turn of Belgrade's *Vecernje novosti*. In the face of widespread protest, the independent daily was summarily placed under state ownership without even the fig-leaf of a court order, thus denying owners Novosti AD any chance of legal redress. Novosti's board conceded that the paper's independence had been lost. On 25 March, Serbia's only newsprint manufacturer ceased production because of what was described as a 'shortage' of pulp and foreign exchange. The shortage was construed by the independents as a further attack on their existence; they are not permitted by law to import paper.

But the toughest measures under the 1998 information act were reserved for Serbia's lively independent radio and television sector. TV Nemanja and Radio Golf were closed down in mid-February on the grounds they had not 'met the conditions' for obtaining licenses. Zoran Malesevic, owner of Radio Senta and Radio VK in Kikinda, was in court on 14 February to face charges of 'operating without a licence' (*Index* 3/1999, 5/1999), though receipts exist to prove that he had paid the necessary fees. On 8 March, Pozarevac's Radio Boum 93 was shut down because it, too, had failed to meet 'the conditions'. On 9 March, two more private outlets, Radio Tir and Nemanja TV in Cuprija were suspended. In Nis, southern Serbia, TV5 faced closure after the Yugoslav Army, which owns its premises, ordered the director to vacate. On 12 March, in defiance of residents' protests, the municipal television station in Pozega was shut down and, on 20 March its director was fined 75,000 dinars (US$6,700) for 'operating without a licence'. The transmission facility on Mount Goc, which belongs to Radio Television Kraljevo, was seized on 17 March for 'operating without a licence'.

In Belgrade, where opposition to Milosevic's rule is stiffer, so too were the attacks on independent stations and the financial penalties against them. Studio B and RadioB2 92 – successor to the original Radio B92 (*Index* 3/1999, 4/1999) – had transmission equipment stolen from their premises in Belgrade after five men in police uniform assaulted the two security guards on 8 March. Within hours, Studio B and its general manager and chief editor, Dragan Kojadinovic, were fined the maximum allowable penalty of 450,000 dinars (US$40,180) for a comment broadcast in a live interview which, the station protests, could not have been prevented. Two hours later, minister of telecommunications Ivan Markovic issued an order for Studio B to pay a massive 10,755,314 dinars (cUS$960,295) for 'frequency fees' within seven days. On 14 March, the private television station had nearly all its debts and fines paid off by Belgrade's city council which, like Studio B itself, is controlled by Vuk Draskovic's Serbian Renewal Movement.

Independent media in Serbia retain a small degree of power to hit back, but tactics are limited. Local committees for the defence of their stations began to operate at the end of March in Nis, Cacak, Pirot, Pozega and Kragujevac while the Association of Professional Journalists of Montenegro announced a show of solidarity with the Independent Association of Serbian Journalists. On 21 March, the European Parliament said it would replace the equipment that had been stolen, but its influence is also circumscribed. Jean-Claude Galli, Belgrade correspondent for France's TF1 and RF, had his accreditation refused and was forced to leave on 22 March, bringing to 80 the number of foreign journalists deported in recent months.

Independent witnesses, both local and foreign, have been removed before whatever comes next. ❑

Michael Griffin & Katy Sheppard

A *censorship chronicle incorporating information from the American Association for the Advancement of Science Human Rights Action Network (AAASHRAN), Amnesty International (AI), Article 19 (A19), Alliance of Independent Journalists (AJI), the BBC Monitoring Service Summary of World Broadcasts (SWB), the Committee to Protect Journalists (CPJ), Canadian Journalists for Free Expression (CJFE), Glasnost Defence Foundation (GDF), Instituto de Prensa y Sociedad (IPYS), The UN's Integrated Regional Information Network (IRIN), the Inter-American Press Association (IAPA), the International Federation of Journalists (IFJ/FIP), Human Rights Watch (HRW), the Media Institute of Southern Africa (MISA), Network for the Defence of Independent Media in Africa (NDIMA), International PEN (PEN), Open Media Research Institute (OMRI), Pacific Islands News Association (PINA), Radio Free Europe/Radio Liberty (RFE/RL), Reporters Sans Frontières (RSF), the World Association of Community Broadcasters (AMARC), World Association of Newspapers (WAN), the World Organisation Against Torture (OMCT) and other sources*

ALGERIA

On 12 February **C Mechakara**, a correspondent of French daily *El Watan* based in Constantine, was fined 1,000 dinars (US$16) and ordered to pay a token one dinar in damages to retired general Mohammed Betchine. The libel case arose from an article by Mechakara about the assassination of the financial director of Constantine district. The correctional court also fined the managing editor of the Arab-

language daily *El Youm* 1,500 dinars for the same libel. (IFJ)

On 28 March the military security branch arrested **Zerog Walid**, a freelance photographer working for the French press agency Imparess, at his home in Algiers' El Biar district. He was detained at Ben Aknoun police barracks after his videotapes and films had been confiscated He was released on 2 April. (RSF)

ANGOLA

Former Angolan National Radio editor and *Folha 8* journalist **Andre Domigos Mussamo** was released on bail on 16 March after three months in illegal detention (*Index* 2/2000). No date has been set for trial and it is unclear if Mussamo has been formally charged. (CPJ)

Freelance journalist **Rafael Marques** was sentenced to six months' jail and fined US$16,000 on 6 April for defaming President Dos Santos and Attorney-General Domingos Culolo (*Index* 6/1999, 1/2000, 2/2000) amid charges that irregularities in the trial rendered the ruling invalid. On 20 March, it was reported that local sources claimed the judge was a former member of the secret police with no formal legal training, while the trial was held in a closed court with Marques forced to represent himself after the judge barred his lawyer, **Luis Nascimento**. Marques was allowed only one witness, whose testimony was dismissed by the judge. Marques has been released on bail, but has been gagged from talking about the case and ordered not to leave the country. (CPJ, Open Society Institute)

Two *Angolense* editors have been convicted of criminal defamation, it was reported on 13 April. News editor **Graca Campos** and editor **Americo Goncalves** were sentenced to four months and three months in prison respectively and ordered to pay US$40,000 compensation. Their sentences were suspended for three years. The charges arose from a series of articles published in 1998 and 1999, which described Kwanza-Norte governor Manuel Pedro Pakavira as 'incompetent'. (WAN)

ARGENTINA

Eight men accused of the brutal murder in 1997 of photojournalist **José Luis Cabezas** were sentenced to life imprisonment on 4 February (*Index* 2/1997, 3/1997, 5/1997, 6/1997). The court also ruled that deceased businessman Alfredo Yabran – who committed suicide in 1998 – arranged the murder after feeling aggrieved over a photograph of him by Cabezas published in the weekly *Noticias*. (IAPA, Periodistas)

Five intelligence air force officers were indicted by a federal court judge on 2 March for illegally snooping on ten journalists who had been investigating security problems at Argentine airports three year ago. The officers are charged with 'abuse of authority' for employing illegal intelligence procedures to investigate **Rolando Barbano**, **Alcadio Oña** and **Hernán Firpo** of daily *Clarín*, **Adrián Ventura**, **Roberto Solans** and **Alfredo Vega** of the daily *La Nación*, **Carlos Rodríguez** and **Sergio Moreno** of the daily *Página/12*, and **José E. Toyah** and **Dolores**

Olveira of *El Cronista*. (Periodistas)

Unidentified gunmen shot at the home of an editorial board member of *La Gaceta de Tucumán* newspaper and local Justicialista Party leader **Bernardo García Hamilton** on 29 March. García was doubtful that the attack had anything to do with his political activities, believing instead that it was provoked by the coverage given by *La Gaceta* of several cases of police corruption. (Periodistas)

Luis Giménez, general secretary of Telám News Agency, was returning home in Buenos Aires on 29 March when he was tipped off about individuals who had been watching his house. Provincial police later stopped some men fitting the description, who identified themselves as federal police. The next day, Giménez was threatened with death. (IFJ)

AUSTRALIA

It was reported on 17 March that evidence of Australia's violation of international human rights conventions were removed from a UN report on mandatory sentencing following pressure from Prime Minister John Howard's government. The report had concluded that laws in the Northern Territory, primarily directed at Aborigines, breached the UN Convention on the Rights of the Child, as well as numerous human rights instruments on racial discrimination. (*www.wsws.org*)

Riot police 'roughed up' journalists covering a demonstration of members of the Building Workers International

Union on 25 February, it was reported on 29 February. An inquiry has been opened. (RSF)

AUSTRIA

It was reported on 24 March that a female cleric, **Bishop Gertraud Knoll**, a fierce critic of Jorg Haider's Freedom Party (FPÖ), has gone into hiding to escape from a campaign of hate mail and abusive calls since she took part in demonstrations against the FPÖ's role in government. (*The Times*)

AZERBAIJAN

Yeni Musavat journalist **Elbeyi Hassanli** was abducted from the newspaper's offices on 7 February on the pretext of being questioned at the local police station about articles critical of President Heidar Aliyev. He was bundled into a car and taken to Nakhichevan Autonomous Republic where he was allegedly tortured. As protests at his abduction grew in Baku, Hassanli was released from Nakhichevan prison on 10 February. His articles in *Yeni Musavat* exposed corruption in Nakhichevan, an exclave of Azeri territory between Armenia, Turkey and Iran that is the power base of President Heidar Aliyev. (Azerbaijan Journalists' Trade Union, SWB)

Later on 7 February a group of about 100 club-wielding men clashed with *Yeni Musavat* journalists at their office building. The men announced that they had arrived from the Nahkichevan village of Nehram to 'settle scores' with the newspaper before smashing windows and equipment. At least

one *Yeni Musavat* journalist was injured by broken glass. (Azerbaijan Journalists' Trade Union, Reuters, RFE/RL, Turan)

On 8 February equipment worth approximately US$120,000, including television transmitters, was taken from the premises of Sara TV. Sara representatives believe the confiscation was ordered by Husein Huseynov, head of the Motor Transport Agency and director of the newly approved, state-supported LTV station. The equipment was allegedly seized in compensation for a fine of 250 million manats (US$62,000) levied against the station in November 1999 (*Index* 6/1999, 1/2000, 2/2000), after it was found guilty of insulting Huseynov's 'honour and dignity'. (CPJ, A19, Sara TV, *Bilik Dunyasi*)

Journalists from several Baku newspapers claimed on 24 February that they had been instructed by the justice ministry not to cover the trial of prisoners involved in what authorities claim was a mutiny at a jail near Baku in January 1999. Prisoners' relatives say the alleged mutiny was staged to facilitate the murder of former **General Vahid Musaev**, serving time for involvement in a 1995 assassination attempt on President Heidar Aliev. (Turan)

A police official who declined to divulge his identity telephoned *Azadlyg* on 15 March and warned that preparations were under way for an attack on the paper's premises. (Turan)

Alem newspaper was fined 5,500,000 manats (about US$1,200) for 'undermining the principles of Islam and corrupting the morals of Azeri youth' in a case brought by a number of Islamic organisations, it was reported on 13 March. (Azerbaijan News Service)

Official registration of the Committee for Democracy and Human Rights and the Trade Union of Journalists was announced by the justice ministry on 23 March and 28 March respectively. (CDHR, TUJo)

Vahram Aghajanian, a journalist for the newspaper *Tasnerord Nahang* (Tenth Province) in Nagorno Karabakh, was jailed for a year on 12 April for defaming Karabakh premier Anushavan Danielian in an article last November which accused Danielian of failing to aid a local village which had strongly criticised him. (Azerbaijan Journalists' Trade Union, IWPR)

The editorial board of *Tasnerord Nahang* issued a statement on 15 April saying that it is suspending publication indefinitely following Aghajanian's 'unfair' trial and sentence and because Karabakh 'society is not prepared' for an opposition publication. (RFE/RL)

BANGLADESH

On 7 March the *Weekly Evidence*, a publication close to the opposition Bangladesh National Party (BNP), was forbidden from being distributed free to public offices. (RSF)

The following day police raided the offices of the daily *Dainik Dinkal*, one of the most important papers controlled by the BNP, in an attempt to arrest

the paper's three managing editors for allegedly insulting a local member of parliament. So far, editor **Akhter-ul-Alam**, managing editor **AKM Mossaraf Hossain** and publisher **Majidul Alam** have not been arrested. (RSF)

On 19 March **Mohiuddin Murad**, a correspondent in Lakhipur with *Dainik Janakantha*, became the first journalist to be charged with 'incitement to violence and rebellion' under the recently adopted Public Safety Act. (RSF)

Recent Publication: *Bangladesh: Human Rights in the Chittagong Hill Tracts* (AI, February 2000, pp 24).

BOSNIA-HERZEGOVINA

The broadcast facilities of Erotel in Mostar were closed down by engineers from the international community's Independent Media Commission on 17 February at the request of the OSCE's Wolfgang Petritsch. Claiming that the station was operating without a licence, Petritsch's spokesman said that the move freed the frequency to allow for a new public television station, mainly for the Croatian and Muslim federation. (RFE/LR)

BRAZIL

Three journalists from the daily *O Povo* in the north-east were arrested and beaten by police on 23 February while investigating reports of corruption in the municipal government of Hidrolandia, Ceará. Local mayor Luis Antonio Farías allegedly instigated and took part in the attack. The victims were reporter

Erick Guimaraes, photographer **Marco Studart** and driver **Valdir Gomez Soares**. Studart and Gomez claim they were tortured during their detention. (IAPA)

CAMBODIA

On 4 April the ministry of information ordered a 30-day suspension of *Pritbat Pordamean Kampuchea*, a new weekly published in English and Khmer since 1 January. The ban followed news stories that allegedly defamed 'members of the Royal Government', although the authorities did not cite any specific article or issue in support of its claims. (CPJ)

CAMEROON

On 23 February Radio Buea in the town of Buea in the south-west broadcast a programme in which a Cameroonian living in England claimed that President Paul Biya's government marginalised English speakers and violated their constitutional rights. Shortly after the broadcast, the station was raided by the police who arrested manager **Chris Oben**, producer **Jean-Mathias Kouemeko** and technician **Theresa Forbin**. All three were released after several hours' interrogation by police. (CPJ)

On 3 April a criminal court in the western town of Bafoussam convicted **Michael Eclador Pekoua**, publisher of the privately owned weekly *Ouest Echos*, of defamation and sentenced him to six months in prison without parole. The verdict came six months after Pekoua was fined 800,000 CFA

Francs (approx. US$170) after a complaint by the state-owned oil company Société Nationale des Hydrocarbures (SNH) that the publisher had defamed two company officials in an August 1999 editorial. Quoting a leaked SNH document, Pekoua had alleged that executive director Adolphe Moduki embezzled large sums of company money, spending much of it on his lover, an executive secretary at SNH. Shortly after publication the authorities asked him to reveal the names of his sources. The journalist refused, citing article of the press law which guarantees protection of sources. (CPJ)

CHAD

Hunting the Dictator, an account by journalist **Daniel Bekoutou** of how his life was threatened after he led the fight to have former president Hissene Habré prosecuted for torture, has been published on the Internet. On 3 February Habré was indicted with much of the evidence against him supplied by Bekoutou, a reporter with the Dakar daily *Walfadjri*. The day after the indictment, Bekoutou began to receive death threats. Fearing for his life, he fled to Paris. (CPJ)

CHECHNYA

The notes, camera, address book and telephone of **Anne Nivat**, special envoy for the French dailies *Ouest-France* and *Libération*, were confiscated by Federal Security Service (FSB) on 10 February, making it impossible for her to contact her editorial offices. The owner of the house where she was staying in Novye Atagui in south Grozny was also

arrested. (RSF, RFE/RL)

At an FSB briefing in Moscow a witness who had been released from Chechnya reported the death of photojournalist **Vladimir Yatsina**, a 20-year veteran of *ITAS-TASS*. Yatsina had been missing since 19 July 1999 when he was reportedly kidnapped in Nazran, Ingushetia, and taken to Chechnya. (CPJ)

CHILE

On 7 February the Supreme Court banned circulation of the free daily *Metro*, distributed in Santiago underground stations since 14 January. The ruling followed a complaint by the National Press Association, which charged that the paper had 'acted unconstitutionally' and harmed the financial interests of dailies affiliated to the association. The court overturned a previous ruling by the Court of Appeals that had acquitted *Metro* of the charges. (IFJ)

On 22 February Chile's Supreme Court upheld a 541-day suspended jail sentence handed down to journalist **José Ale** of the Santiago daily *La Tercera* that had been previously revoked by the Court of Appeals. The former editor of *La Tercera*, **Fernando Paulsen**, was acquitted. Both Ale and Paulsen were tried under the notorious State Security Law of 1958 in connection with defamation charges filed by Supreme Court minister Judge Servando Jordán, who objected to an article published in January 1998 alleging a rift between him and the Supreme Court presidency. (IFJ)

CHINA

Falun Gong adherents continue to fall foul of the authorities in numbers too great to record in individual detail here. Eleven members of the so-called 'cult' are confirmed as having died in police custody. For fully-referenced information about the victims of the crackdown, please see *www.indexoncensorship.org /news/*

News emerged on 12 February of the arrest of four writers associated with the underground literary magazine *China Cultural Revival Bulletin*, founded in 1997 to advocate freeing artists and writers from the constraints of party ideology. The editors, poet **Xiong Jinren** and his partner **Chen Wei**, were arrested on 11 January in Guiyang, Guizhou Province. **Wang Yiliang**, a freelance writer, and **Hu Jun**, a professor at a Shanghai college of management, were arrested in Shanghai on 20 January. All were sentenced without trial to three years in labour camps. The magazine's co-founder, **Ma Zhe**, has spent the last two years in detention without charge while police in Guiyang gathered evidence against him for 'subversively advocating that literary creations cast off Communist ideology'. He was tried and sentenced on 1 March to five years in prison. (Agence-France Presse, Associated Press, Information Centre of Human Rights and Democratic Movements in China)

On 10 February **Archbishop John Yang Shudao** was arrested by 100 armed police at midnight on charges relating to his continued loyalty to Rome. His

• •

LOIS WHEELER SNOW
Distant ashes

31 March: I have come to China to visit my husband's grave at Beijing University. While in Beijing I want very much to call on Professor Ding Zilin (*Index*, 3/1999). I understand that she is under surveillance but I trust this will not prevent my visit. It is a visit from a mother with her son to extend sympathy to a mother who has lost her son, and to bring her whatever solace we can. It is also a gesture of solidarity with the other mothers and families who, more than ten years ago now, had their loved ones taken from them in the violence of Tiananmen and who, as a result, have been deprived of normal lives and liberties.

My visit is undertaken in [the] spirit of friendship my husband and I have always had for the valiant Chinese people, a friendship which began with Edgar Snow in the early years of China's struggle to create a better society and which I have steadily maintained since his death.

1 April
Dear Premier Zhu Rongji,
This morning, my son and I were prevented from entering the grounds of People's University and visiting Professor Ding Zilin. The reason given was that permission was needed from higher authorities. I am therefore writing directly to you in the hope that you will give this matter your personal attention and make it possible for me to meet Mrs Ding before my departure on 4 April.

4 April
I leave China with a heavy heart. I deeply regret that my request for permission to visit Ding Zilin has gone unanswered, and I am appalled that Mrs Ding's friend, Su Bingxian, was detained for questioning after speaking to me. I appeal to the authorities to cease the harassment of these two women and of the families of all the victims of the 1989 violence at Tiananmen. The violation of [their] rights by the government, while Edgar Snow's ashes lie buried in Beijing University, makes a mockery of all that he stood for. I can only hope that the authorities will have the foresight not to put me in a position where I will have to reconsider the appropriateness of leaving them there. ❏

Lois Wheeler Snow, 79, is the widow of the noted sinologist Edgar Snow. **Ding Zilin**, *63, has been the driving force behind the documentation of the victims of the Tiananmen massacre and a member of the June Fourth Mothers group. The full text of these letters is available on* www.hrichina.org/pr/english/000403a.htm

• •

refusal to accept Beijing's authority over China's Catholics has seen him spend over 30 of his 84 years in prisons and labour camps. Scores of priests and lay-persons are being held in jails and camps, as are at least eight bishops, named as **An Shuxin**, **Han Dingxiang**, **Jia Zhiguo**, **Lin Xili**, **Su Zhimin**, **Xie Shiguang**, **Zhang Weizhu** and **Yang Shudao**. On 2 March 16 members of China Evangelistic Fellowship, a Christian group branded an 'evil cult', were arrested in Xinyang, Henan Province. One of those detained was **Jiang Qinggang**, who has already served two terms in labour camps for his beliefs, the most recent of which finished two months ago. (Agence-France Presse, Associated Press, Information Centre of Human Rights and Democratic Movements in China)

The 14-year-old **Karmapa Lama**, who recently fled Tibet (*Index* 2/2000), said on 19 February: 'Tibet, where great religions and cultures have flourished in the past is facing a great threat of extinction.' On 1 March it was reported that the Karmapa's parents had been detained by police investigating his escape to India. Beijing denies the report, claiming they have merely left Lhasa to 'tend livestock' elsewhere in Tibet. (Tibet Information Network, Agence-France Presse, Associated Press)

Liu Shizun, former assistant to the jailed China Democracy Party (CDP) co-founder, **Xu Wenli** (*Index* 2/1999, 5/1999), has been jailed for six years on charges of subversion in Dalian, Liaoning Province. Xu Wenli's wife, **He**

Xintong, undertook a 24-hour hunger strike to coincide with the arrival of the UN High Commissioner on Human Rights, Mary Robinson, in Beijing on 2 March. At least four other CDP activists were taken into custody for the duration of Robinson's visit from 2 to 4 March. (Agence-France Presse, Associated Press, Information Centre of Human Rights and Democratic Movements in China, Human Rights in China, *VIP Reference*)

Zhong Gong, a banned group similar in beliefs to Falun Gong (*Index* 2/2000), submitted an open letter of protest on 13 March to President Jiang Zemin and the National People's Congress. They demanded the release of 600 members arrested since October 1999 and the return of US$10 million in funds and assets confiscated when 3,000 legally registered enterprises were closed. Additionally, they claim 12,000 people have lost their jobs as a direct result of the group being banned – allegedly on the direct orders of Jiang Zemin. (Agence-France Presse, Associated Press, Information Centre of Human Rights and Democratic Movements in China, Human Rights in China, *VIP Reference*)

On 11 March **Rabiya Kadeer**, a Muslim businesswoman from China's restive north-western Xinjiang Province (*Index* 6/1999), was sentenced to eight years in prison on vague charges of endangering state security, probably relating to newspaper clippings she sent to her husband in the US. (Agence-France Presse, Associated Press, AI)

In what appears to be a renewed clampdown on reformist intellectuals, on 7 April four well-known 'pro-west' writers had their work banned from appearing in official publications. **Li Shenzhi**, **Mao Yushi**, **Fan Gang** and **Liu Junning** have written extensively on issues of political and economic reform and it is reported that their works were compiled into a volume of 'objectionable bourgeois-liberal writings' by the state propaganda department. (*South China Morning Post, Hong Kong Standard*)

Cameraman **John Restrepo Abello** of a local television channel in Barrancabermeja was found murdered in his brother's home in Girón, Santander province. The attack – in which Restrepo's brother also died – was perpetrated by unknown individuals on 5-6 February. No motive was reported. (Prensa Libre, IFJ)

National Liberation Army (ELN) guerrillas allegedly stopped and burned two press vehicles on 11 February belonging to radio stations RCN and Radio Caracol, endangering the lives of two unnamed journalists. The assailants – allegedly from the splinter guerrilla group of Carlos Alberto Buitrago – attacked the two vehicles after blocking the highway between the cities of Bogotá and Medellín in protest of what they see as a government and army dominated press. (Prensa Libre, IFJ)

Journalist **Antonio Gómez Gómez** was shot dead on 9 February in front of his wife and daughter by a gang of hooded assailants. The 60-year-old journalist was the owner of Ecos de la Sierra (Echos from the Highlands) radio station in Palmor, which he used to promote community action campaigns. (Prensa Libre, IFJ)

Journalist **María Elena Salinas Gallego**, reported missing on 2 March, was found dead three days later in a correctional centre in San Carlos, Antioquia, next to the bodies of two ELN guerrillas killed in a confrontation with troops. Salinas, a professor at Medellín University's Faculty of Social Communications and freelance journalist, went missing after travelling to San Carlos to investigate the armed conflict there. (IFJ)

Television host **Fernando Gonzales Pacheco** has fled the country after revealing on 6 March that he had received death threats. The veteran presenter, who has hosted numerous game shows and news programmes, did not reveal any further details. (IFJ)

Francisco 'Pacho' Santos Calderón, editor of the daily *El Tiempo*, fled the country on 11 March. Santos was heading towards his favourite restaurant when his bodyguards noticed that a number of cars that had been trailing the journalist for the past month were parked outside. The editor founded the only NGO dedicated to ending kidnapping. (CPJ, RSF)

Mireya Alvarez Ramírez, owner and editor of newspaper *La Palma de Facetas* in Palma-Cundinamarca region, has gone into exile a second time because of threats against her life. Alvarez was given until 20 March to pay ten million pesos (about US$5,000) or face death. (IFJ)

Journalist **Humberto Good Garcés** was murdered on 8 March by unknown gunmen who shot him five times in a disco. The assailants took Good's car and later abandoned it, tearing up his Reporters sans Frontières membership card. (IFJ)

On 13 April two men entered the offices of *Alternativa* in Bogotá and asked to see **Fabio Castillo**, one of two editors. When Castillo's assistant said he was unavailable, one of the men held a large knife to her throat while the other grabbed the arm of a reporter who was the only other person in the office. After locking the two employees in a bathroom, the men ransacked the office, taking documents, computer disks and a list of subscribers. A feature story in the current issue chronicles an alleged plot through which ultra-right political forces planned to seize power. (CPJ)

COTE D'IVOIRE

Three armed soldiers stormed the offices of independent daily *Soir Info* on 5 March, interrogating its publisher **Ferro Bi**. The soldiers wanted to speak to **Alain Bouabre** and **Claude Daasse**, authors of an article critical of salary and work conditions at a state-owned timber company. The soldiers held Bi for over an hour, interrogating him about the newspaper's 'hidden agenda'. (CPJ)

Ten soldiers raided the offices of *Le National* and attacked its staff on 24 March. The incident was reportedly prompted by an editorial in that day's edition which criticised President Robert Guei's governing style. (CPJ)

CROATIA

The contents of the documents in possession of the late Franjo Tudjman are to be made public by the new President Stipe Mesic, who said in Pula on 14 March that only documents containing military secrets would remain classified. (RFE/RL)

CUBA

Journalist **Angel Pablo Polanco**, director of the *Noticuba* agency, was arrested on 23 February while preparing to cover the 25 February trial of **Oscar Elias Biscet**. Polanco had previously published a number of articles on the judicial proceedings against **Biscet**. On 22 February **Omar Rodriguez Saludes** of the *New Press Agency* was detained for four hours. (RSF)

On 27 February **Doctor Oscar Elías Biscet González** was sentenced to three years' imprisonment after being arrested for hanging the national flag sideways at a press conference. The physician, who is president of the Lawton Human Rights Foundation, said that patriots have always used the tactic as a sign of civil disobedience. Biscet is accused of insulting the nation's symbols, public disorder and inciting criminal activity. (AI, RSF)

There is increasing concern for the health of writer and political activist **Marta Beatriz Roque Cabello**, who is suffering from a condition that could be cancerous. The writer is halfway through a three-year sentence and is already in poor health. She was arrested along with three others on charges of 'sedition and other acts against state security' for an article entitled *La Patria es de Todos*, co-authored by **Felix Antonio Bonne Cascasses, Rene Gomez Manzano** and **Vladimir Roca Antunez**. (PEN)

DEMOCRATIC REPUBLIC OF CONGO

On 16 February **Richard Nsamba Olangi Diata**, publisher of the pro-government Kinshasa newspaper *Le Messager Africain*, was arrested by five members of the Congolese National Police's (PNC) special services and taken to jail in Kinshasa/Gombe. During a threatening interrogation, Nsmaba was accused of 'insulting' Interior Minister Gaetan Kaukudji. He was released on 18 February after the PNC told Nsamba that Kaukudji intended to prohibit *Le Messenger Africain*. (Journaliste en Danger)

Ntumba Lumembu Monji Mule, a journalist with the Kinshasa weekly *Umoja*, was detained at his residence by four PNC agents on 21 January. After refusing to leave with the agents, two went to fetch a summons for 'refusal to testify'. The arrest concerned an article, entitled 'Teshisekedi escapes death', published in the 15 February edition of *Umoja*. The journalist later proved to police that he had not in fact written the article, but another journalist **Katambwa Mike Masiya**. Ntumba was released. (Journaliste en Danger)

Freddy Loseke Lisumba la

Yayenga, publisher of the Kinshasa newspaper *La Libre Afrique*, is reported to be suffering from beatings in his prison at the headquarters of the Seventh Military Region, located in Kinshasa/Badalungwa (*Index* 2/2000). (Journaliste en Danger, CPJ)

On 11 March the director-general of the Bureau of Illegally Acquired Goods (OBMS) presented a court order to private Radio Television Kin Malebo (RTKM) calling for the requisition of its offices, equipment and furniture. No reason was given for the action. RTKM belongs to **Aubain Ngongo Luwowo**, minister of information under Mobutu, who currently lives in exile. The station has a long-standing reputation for independent reporting. The OBMS is responsible for the 'management' of assets seized from officials of the deposed regime of Mobutu. (Journaliste en Danger)

Journalist **Nyembo Kimuni**, of the Lumbagu private weekly *La Tribune*, was arrested at home on 13 March by agents of the National Information Agency (ANR). He is accused of publishing an article about security in Katanga in which it was written that 'the ANR/Katanga is a lair of terror and extortion and reprisals'. (RSF)

On 3 April journalist **Joseph-Boucard Kasonga Tshilunde Baya Yowunwe**, publisher of the Kinshasa paper *L'Eveil*, was summoned by the crime squad of the public prosecutor's office's criminal investigation department in Kinshasa, but requested to

return on Tuesday 4 April. The reason for the investigation is unknown. (Journaliste en Danger)

ECUADOR

The head of Telecentro Televisión news programme, **Rafael Cuesta**, suffered superficial wounds to his face and hands while opening a letter bomb addressed to him on 16 February. The anonymous letter was mailed from the city of Cuenca, in Azuay province. Meanwhile, journalists **Andrés Carrión** and **Gonzalo Ortiz Crespo**, from Telesistema and Gamavisión TV channels respectively, have been receiving threatening letters since 21 January from a previously unknown guerrilla group named the National Liberation Army (ELN). (RSF)

EGYPT

On 1 February the daily *Al Akhbar* reported the imminent publication of a draft law which gives the Cabinet powers to cancel the licence of a newspaper on the grounds of 'moral corruption, assault on religions, upsetting of public security, disseminating horror among people and causing harm to public interest'. (Egyptian Organisation For Human Rights)

On 13 February **Hafez Abu Seada**, secretary of the Egyptian Organisation For Human Rights, was referred to the Emergency Supreme State Security for breaching military order 4/1992 which forbids acceptance of monetary donations from foreign countries without prior permission. Abu Saeda's referral is linked to the donation of £25,000 (US$39,500) from the Human Rights Committee of the British parliament for projects for women and the disabled. (A19, Egyptian Organisation For Human Rights)

On 1 April Cairo Criminal Court sentenced four journalists to varying terms of prisons along with fines (*Index* 3/1998, 4/1998, 5/1998. 6/1998, 4/1999, 5/1999). **Magdhy Hussein**, editor-in-chief of *Al Shaab*, and reporter **Saleh Bedewi** were each sentenced to two years'jail. The paper's cartoonist, **Essam Eddine Hanafi**, was given one year in prison. The fourth defendant, publisher **Adel Hussein**, was fined US$5,900, as were the other three. This drawn-out case began in 1998 when the paper accused the deputy prime minister and agricultural minister, Yusuf Wali, of increasing co-operation with Israel. Since then it has zigzagged through a series of sentences and appeals. The decision has been appealed. (CPJ, Egyptian Organisation For Human Rights)

ETHIOPIA

It was reported on 28 January that **Dawit Kebede**, a member of the executive committee of the Ethiopian Free Press Association, had fled to Kenya to evade at least ten pending legal charges against him. (IFJ)

Abera Wogi, editor-in-chief of the private weekly *Maebel*, was released from Addis Ababa's Kerhiele prison in mid-February on completion of his one-year sentence for 'propagating false news' (*Index* 2/2000). Also released on bail was **Bizunesh**

Kebede, editor-in-chief of *Zegabi*. The exact date of her release is unknown. (RSF)

After 11 years, the Ethiopian Free Press Association (EFAJ) was officially recognised by the Justice Ministry on 13 March. (CPJ, IFJ)

FIJI

Thakur Ranjit Singh, a Radio Fiji presenter, was removed from his post after Prime Minister Mahendra Chaudry accused him of being biased against his Labour Party, it was reported on 17 March. Singh is publisher of the *Daily Post*, in which the government has the biggest share. (PINA)

It was reported on 27 February that Assistant Minister for Information Lekh Rram Vayeshnoi has filed a writ against Fiji Television. He alleges that the station damaged his reputation by broadcasting claims he was unfit to hold office. (Pacific Media Watch)

Government backbench MP Muthu Swamy, who made allegations over the personal and professional integrity of three *Fiji Times* journalists last November (*Index* 1/2000), threatened on 26 February to sue the *Daily Post* for publishing a photograph of him asleep in the House during a debate. Swamy claimed he had his head down reading the bill at the time. (Pacific Media Watch)

GAMBIA

Radio journalist **Omar Barrow** was shot dead by anti-riot police during a violent student demonstration on 10 April. Barrow, a SUD FM news editor,

was shot in the armpit twice while he worked in the Red Cross compound as a first-aid volunteer. Eleven others were killed during the riot which was called to protest against the alleged murder of a student by a fire department employee and the reported rape of a 13-year-old girl by a police officer. (CPJ)

GEORGIA

After a campaign of threats and intimidation from parliamentary deputy Aslan Smirba, three of the four owners of the Batumi independent TV station, Telekanal 25, were forced to sign over their shares to Mikhail Gagoshidze on 19 February. Smirba, a former mayor of Batumi, reportedly punched Telekanal 25 business director **Atandil Gvasaliya** and threatened to 'put a bullet through someone's head' unless the shares were transferred to Gagoshidze, his nominee. (Internews, CPJ, *Segodnya*)

A hearing into the alleged assault of two journalists by Tbilisi traffic police began at the end of February. The incident happened in October 1999 when **Georgi Kapanadzee**, a journalist with the newspaper *Resonansi*, intervened to help a person reportedly severely beaten by the police. He ended up in Tbilisi's Hospital No. 1 with concussion. **Sergey Balousov**, the paper's photographer, had his camera confiscated when he attempted to take pictures of the police. (AI)

On 29 February a Tbilisi district court rejected an appeal by parliamentary deputy Guram Sharadze to revoke the legal registration of the Jehovah's

Witnesses (*Index* 1/2000). Sharadze's argument that the sect is 'anti-national' and directed against the Orthodox Church was rejected by the court. (*Caucasus Press*)

GREECE

On 3 March world-renowned violinist **Leonidas Kavakos** was given a four-month suspended prison sentence for defamation of three members of the artistic board of the Salonica State Orchestra. He was ordered to pay a fine of 200,000 drs (approximately US$600) in damages to each of the plaintiffs. The statements were made by Kavakos during a March 1999 interview in a local newspaper. (Greek Helsinki Monitor)

On 3 March novelist **Mimis Androulakis** and his publisher **Thanasis Kastaniotis** were indicted by a Salonica prosecutor for 'committing blasphemy against a religion and its founder'. In Androulakis' new book, *M to the Nth Power*, he presents Jesus Christ as having sexual relationships and children out of wedlock. (Greek Helsinki Monitor)

On 7 March composer **Manolis Rasoulis** was given a 12-month prison sentence for defamatory statements about singer Yorgos Dalara that he made in an interview to the daily *Exousia* on 14 April 1998. Rasoulis claimed that Dalara had not performed at a benefit concert for free, but was paid. Rasoulis was tried *in absentia* since he had left Greece on the previous day 'for ever'. (Greek Helsinki Monitor)

GUATEMALA

On 28 February charges were dropped against Jóse Obdulio Villanueva, a former member of the presidential military guard, who was a suspect in the 26 April 1998 murder of Bishop **Juan José Gerardi**, director of the Archbishop's Office for Human Rights (*Index* 4/1998). The charges were dropped when evidence was produced showing that Villanueva had actually been in jail at the time. In another twist, Catholic priest **Mario Orantes** was rearrested on 9 February (*Index* 2/1999). On 15 February special prosecutor **Leopoldo Zeissig** claimed that he and colleagues investigating the case have received harassing telephone calls. The investigation has been criticised for focusing on robbery or a 'crime of passion' as motives for the murder, rather than retaliation by the military. Gerardi was killed two days after presenting a church report claiming the army was responsible for 93% of the human rights violations during the nation's 36-year civil war. (*Mesoamerica*, BBC, Derechos)

GUINEA

On 7 April **Abdoulaye Sankara**, editor-in-chief of the private weekly *Le Soleil*, was arrested and accused of 'launching a new newspaper' – *Le Soleil Enchainé* – in defiance of a one-month ban imposed on the former publication and the newspaper *L'Oeil* after complaints from businessmen accused of wrongdoing in various articles on 31 March. All copies of *Le Soleil Enchainé*'s first edition were seized. (RSF)

INDIA

On 3 February the Indian Council for Historical Research (ICHR) told Oxford University Press that the 1940 and 1946 volumes of the *Towards Freedom* series, edited by historians **KN Panikkar** and **Sumit Sarkar**, were being withdrawn from press for fresh 'perusal'. According to the ICHR, previous volumes had been of 'dubious quality', and it appeared that Panikkar and Sarkar had 'unscrupulously' deleted vital paragraphs, 'in utter disregard for the well-accepted norms of editing'. After the initial recriminations had died down, it emerged that Hindu nationalism rather than acadmic objectivity was the real reason for the furore. According to reports, members of the Rashtriya Sewak Sanjh – the religious ideologues behind the governing Hindu nationalist Bharatiya Janata Party – had pressured ICHR chairman BR Grover, himself a member of the fundamentalist Vishwa Hindu Parishad, to halt publication of the volumes because they were upset that their members were accurately shown to have not been very active in the freedom struggle against the British. (*Frontline*)

On 16 February customs agents at Calcutta airport blocked the distribution of 3,000 issues of *Time* magazine because it contained a one-page interview with **Gopal Godse**, the brother of Mohandas Gandhi's assassin, Nathuram Godse. (CPJ)

On 10 March the Punjab authorities withdrew the press accreditation of **Sukbir Singh Osan**, who works for various newspapers and edits the Sikh website *www.burningpunjab.com.* (*RSF*)

Bengali novelist Sunil Gangopadhyay accused film-maker **Deepa Mehta** on 23 March of lifting words, phrases and passages directly from the English translation of his novel *Shei Samai* (Those Days) and using them in the script of her film *Water*. Mehta denied the charge and filed a defamation suit in the Delhi High Court against Gangopadhyay, his publisher and the English translator. Since Mehta's production of *Water* was forced to leave Varanasi by Hindu supremacists in early February (*Index* 2/00), it has been dogged by controversy in Uttar Pradesh – when attempts were made to re-locate there – and in West Bengal, where filming is shortly supposed to recommence. (*Asian Age, Frontline, Sunday Telegraph*)

INDONESIA

On 3 February three members of the Portuguese SIC television station – reporter **Joao Ferreira**, news editor **Rita Nolasco** and cameraman **Fernando Faria** – were arrested near Kefamenanutaken in West Timor for not having a special permit, although they had journalists' visas from the consulate in Darwin and had registered with police in the West Timor town of Motoain. They had been interviewing Moko Soares, head of the Sakunar militia, which is accused of committing atrocities against East Timorese civilians who voted for independence. The interview took place just across the border from the East Timor town of Passabe, where UN investigators have discovered mass graves containing the

remains of at least 50 people. The crew believes they were harassed for reporting on the links between the militia leader, the Indonesian military and the police. (CPJ)

On 13 February **Doni Prasetya**, a journalist for *Kediri Pos*, was arrested and questioned for ten hours at Polres police station in Tulungagung, eastern Java, about an article in the 27 January edition in which he implicated a police officer in a corruption case. (RSF)

Yayus Yuswoprihanto a photojournalist for online daily *Detik.com*, was brutally assaulted by police officers on 15 February while covering a demonstration in Jakarta protesting against a courtesy visit by UN General Secretary Kofi Annan. Yayus was hit with rubber sticks, sustaining injuries to the eyes and nose. (AJI)

On 16 February pro-Indonesia mobs attacked the facilities of Radio Republic Indonesia (RRI) and the daily newspaper *Irja Pos* in Merauke and Fakfak, West Papua, following a demonstration against an autonomy package implemented in Merauke. The people, armed with knives, bows and swords, violently attacked the state-owned radio station, effectively putting it out of action. (AJI)

On 23 February journalist **Dani Rahman** of *Memo Arema* was attacked by Syaiful, a member of Tim Reformasi Kecamatan Ngantang. The incident occurred in a small business co-operative area, called Koperasi Unit Desa (KUD), in Sumber Makmur, Malang, East Java. Rahman was reporting on corruption in the

KUD. He arranged to interview Pamudji, KUD's head, about the case but was hindered from leaving by three men, including Syaiful. They demanded that Rahman disclose his source for the story and, when he refused, Syaiful kicked and beat him until he talked. (AJI)

Jakarta News FM radio journalist **Hais Quraisi** was attacked by police on 3 February while reporting on a demonstration outside the attorney general's office in South Jakarta, it was reported on 24 February. The demonstration, aimed at bringing ex-president Suharto to justice, ended in a clash between students and police. Hais was reporting live by mobile phone on the situation. Police officers, dissatisfied with his report, began beating Hais with rattan sticks. (AJI)

On 9 March in Samarinda, East Kalimantan, **Hoesin**, a journalist for *Menara,* was kidnapped and tortured by unidentified assailants. Hoesin was on his way to the governor's office when two men pushed him into a car where three other men were waiting. They drove him round the city while interrogating him, beating him and accusing him of spreading information on a forestry fund corruption case in East Kalimantan. They eventually released him, but the next day he received a death threat. (AJI)

Sigit Tri Pamungkas, a photographer from the *Libero* tabloid, was beaten by PDIP security men in Solo on 12 March as he was taking pictures of a soccer match. (AJI)

On 22 March President Wahid

IRIS OIFIGIUIL
Bookends

*A*dam and Eve, Shaw Desmond, 26 February 1954; *Birth Control Today* Marie Carmichael Stopes, 14 April 1959; *The Book of Love* Upton Sinclair, 16 August 1935; *Boy's Questions Answered* 16 March 1973; *Change of Life in Men and Women* Marie Stopes, 10 October 1952; *Children by Desire* Anne Phelps, 19 February 1935; *Collins Family Medical Encyclopaedia* George Somerville MD, 13 May 1955; *Common Sense about Sex* Leonora Eyles, 26 June 1934; *The Cost of English Morals* Janet Chance, 8 December 1931; *The Encyclopaedia of Sex Practice* Drs A Willy, L Vander, A. Fisher and others, 25 November 1958; *Four Essays on Sex* Havelock Ellis, 9 February 1940; *Family Limitation* Margaret Sanger, 13 May 1930; *Happy Families* William Shadworth, 31 May 1932; *A History of Sex* Simone de Beauvoir, 14 November 1961; *How to be Happy though Human* W Beran Wolfe MD, 19 February 1935; *How to be Happy though Married* W Beran Wolfe MD, 21 May 1954; *Human Sterilisation Today* Cora Hodson, 12 June 1942; *Male Methods of Birth Control* George Ryley Scott, 4 August 1972; *Marriage for Moderns* Barbara Cartland, 20 January 1956; *Marriage and Morals* Bertrand Russell, 20 May 1930; *Marriage, Past, Present and Future* Ralph De Pomerai, 20 November 1931; *The Modern Woman's Medical Guide* 20 April 1951; *Nature of the Second Sex* Simone de Beauvoir, 10 September 1963; *The New Art of Love* George Ryley Scott, 9 September 1958; *Newnes Family Health Encyclopaedia* George Somerville, 21 January 1955; *Old Moore's Almanac 1951*, 20 March 1951; *The Perfect Wife* Dr G Courtenay Beale, 17 July 1936; *The Physiology of Sex* Kenneth Walker, 2 October 1930 *Psychoanalysis and Love* André Tridon, 20 June 1952; *Roman Catholic Methods of Birth Control* Marie Stopes, 18 August 1933; *Sex Morality Tomorrow* Kenneth Ingram, 26 February 1954; *Sexual Behaviour and the Kinsey Report* Morris L Ernst and David Loth, 19 June 1953; *Sexual Behaviour; Psycho-Legal Aspects* Frank S Caprio MD and Donald R Brenner LLB, 17 October 1967; *Sex Ethics* John Ellison, Aubrey Goodwin, Charles Read and Carnac Rivett, 25 December 1934; *Sex, Love and Eugenics* Professor RG Van Yelyr, 20 February 1951; *Sex-Morality Tomorrow* Kenneth Ingram, 26 February 1954; *Sex Problems and Dangers in War Time* George Riley Scott, 13 February 1942; *Sex, Sin and Society* Sydney Hyam, 5 September 1961; *She Looks at Sex* Dr Arlette Fribourg, 4 May 1965; *A Student's Manual of Birth Control* Lily C Butler, 10 December 1937; *Work, Wealth and Happiness of Mankind* HG Wells, 21 June 1932. ❏

The official gazette of the Irish government, Iris Oifigiúil, *published a full list of 420 books that were 'unbanned' on 7 March. This is an edited selection* sacked **Parni Hadi**, head of the official news agency Antara, following complaints from Australian diplomats that he had published 'fiercely anti-Australian' stories during the referendum process in East Timor. Hadi, who had close connections to former president Habibie, was replaced by columnist and writer Mohamad Sobary. On 23 March, Hadi launched a protest against the daily *Sydney Morning Herald* for questioning Antara's accuracy. (Pacific Media Watch)

IRAN

On 5 February political cartoonist **Nik Ahang-Kosar**, of the reformist daily *Azad*, was arrested and called before Tehran's Press Court. The judge criticised two 'insulting' caricatures of conservative dignitary Ayatollah Mohammad-Taghi Mesbah-Yazdi. Ahang-Kosar is being detained at Evine prison and could be sentenced to between a month and one year in prison as well as receiving 74 lashes. (RSF)

On 12 March leading reformist newspaper publisher **Saeed Hajjarian** (*Index* 2/2000) was shot in the face by two unknown assailants on a 1,000cc motorcycle. Under the law, such high-powered motorcycles may only be used by the security forces. Hajjarian, an adviser to President Mohammad Khatami and the editor and publisher of *Sobh-e Emrooz*, is a former hard-liner who participated in the storming of the US embassy in Tehran in 1979. Eight legal complaints had been filed against him since his paper implicated intelligence ministry officials in

the recent 'serial killing' of reformist intellectuals (*Index* 1/1999). Following the assassination attempt, Information Minister Ali Younessi forbade the press from publishing 'any unofficial information, rumours, as well as the foreign press' tendentious analyses of Hajjarian's attackers'. Most reformist papers ignored the ban, resulting in **Emadoldin Baghi** of the daily *Fath* and **Mohammed-Reza Khatami** (the brother of President Khatami) of the daily *Mocherakat*, appearing before the Revolutionary Press Court on 2 and 5 April respectively. (RSF, *International Herald Tribune, Independent*)

Hamid-Reza Kaviani of the weekly *Asr-e-ma* is due to appear before the Special Court for the Clergy on 28 June, because of his book *The Pursuit of the Criminals*, an investigation into the killing of reformist intellectuals in late 1998. Most of the information in the book had already been published in *Asr-e-ma*. (RSF)

Four of 13 Iranian Jews charged with spying for Israel allegedly confessed at a court hearing in Shiraz, southern Iran, on 13 April. However, the trial was closed to the media and western diplomats and defence attorney Ismail Nasseri denied any confessions had been made. (*Guardian*)

IRAQ

A journalist jailed in the 1980s for spying for Saudi Arabia has died in prison, according a 17 April report from his friends. **Najm al-Sadoon**, 83, was Baghdad correspondent for the Saudi daily

Al-Riyad when he was arrested in 1986 and charged with spying. A revolutionary court sentenced him to death but this was commuted to life imprisonment by Saddam Hussein. (Associated Press, Freedom Forum)

ISRAEL

On 31 February the government released the complete memoirs of **Adolf Eichmann**, after a request from Deborah Lipstadt, the US writer fighting a libel action by the alleged Holocaust-denier and British historian David Irving. In the 39 years since they were written in an Israeli prison cell, the notes had 'been read by no more than a handful of specialists'. Attorney-General Elyakim Rubinstein said the state was duty-bound 'to help those who are fighting the denial of the Holocaust'. (*Washington Post*)

Detained Lebanese freelance journalist **Cosette Elias Ibrahim** (*Index* 6/1999) was taken from Khiam in Israeli-occupied southern Lebanon for hospital treatment in the town of Marjayoun following alleged torture, it was reported on 14 March. She has not been charged with any crime, but is believed to be held, along with 174 other Lebanese in Israeli-run jails, as a 'bargaining chip'. (Agence-France Presse)

JAPAN.

The press was incensed at the news blackout which followed the collapse of Prime Minister Keizo Obuchi, who was taken to hospital at 1am on 2 April. The first press conference was not held until 11.30pm. Even then, it was only revealed that Obuchi was

Simon Davies on PRIVACY

Ursula Owen on HATE SPEECH

Patricia Williams on RACE

Edward Lucie-Smith on THE INTERNET

Gabriel Garcia Marquez on JOURNALISM

...all in INDEX

○ **Yes! I want to subscribe to *Index*.**

❏ **1 year (6 issues)**   **£39**   **Save 28%**
❏ **2 years (12 issues)**   **£74**   **Save 31%**
❏ **3 years (18 issues)**   **£102**   <u>**You save 37%**</u>

Name

Address

B9B2

£ _____ enclosed. ❏ Cheque (£)   ❏ Visa/MC   ❏ Am Ex   ❏ Bill me
(*Outside of the UK, add £6 a year for foreign postage*)

Card No.

Expiry   **Signature**

❏ I do not wish to receive mail from other companies.

INDEX

✉ Freepost: INDEX, 33 Islington High Street, London N1 9BR
☎ (44) 171 278 2313   Fax: (44) 171 278 1878
e tony@indexoncensorship.org

SUBSCRIBE & SAVE

North America

○ **Yes! I want to subscribe to *Index*.**

❏ **1 year (6 issues)**   **$52**   **Save 21%**
❏ **2 years (12 issues)**   **$96**   **Save 27%**
❏ **3 years (18 issues)**   **$135**   <u>**You save 32%**</u>

Name

Address

B0B3

$ _____ enclosed. ❏ Cheque ($)   ❏ Visa/MC   ❏ Am Ex   ❏ Bill me

Card No.

Expiry   **Signature**

❏ I do not wish to receive mail from other companies.

INDEX

✉ INDEX, 708 Third Avenue, 8th Floor, New York, NY 10017
☎ (44) 171 278 2313   Fax: (44) 171 278 1878
e tony@indexoncensorship.org

suffering from fatigue, when in fact he had suffered a stroke and was in intensive care. (*Washington Post Service*.)

The Japanese Defence Agency announced on 1 March that it was delaying the installation of a new computer system after discovering some of the software was developed by members of the Aum Shinrikyo cult. The Japan Electronic Computer Co Ltd notified the agency that members of the cult were employed by a sub-contractor. The cult publicly disowned itself from the former leader, Shoko Asahara, in January, changed their name to Aleph and urged members to become law-abiding citizens (*Index* 1/2000, 2/2000). (BBC.)

KAZAKHSTAN

Mangistau Region Governor Lyazzat Kiinov has banned journalists from attending government meetings, Khabar TV reported on 7 March, because they 'deter many from voicing their critical remarks and proposals to each other'. (RFE/RL)

On 31 March TV station Kanal 31 apparently acceded to government pressure by dismissing **Tatiana Deltsova**, the editor-in-chief of the daily news programme *Informbureau*. Kanal 31's director Armanzhan Baytasov has not identified who pressured him, because he 'fears reprisals'. (Internews, RFE/RL)

KENYA

On 7 February police raided Citizen Radio (*Index* 2/2000) in an apparent attempt to intimidate proprietor **Samuel K Macharia**

and his general manager, **Karanja Njoroge**, but left when local and international media rushed to cover the event. The two proprietors had refused to switch off the radio and television as ordered by the Communication Commission of Kenya which accused them of shifting their transmitter. (Rights News Service.)

On 16 February reporter **Johann Wandetto** (*Index* 3/1994, 4/1995, 5/1995, 2/1997, 3/1999), from the daily *People* newspaper in Kitale, Rift Valley Province, was sentenced to 18 months in prison on what the court described as an 'alarmist report' in the 6 March 1999 edition, entitled 'Militia men rob eight crack unit officers: Shock as Moi's men surrender meekly'. The article had claimed that elite presidential guards had been ambushed by cattle rustlers in remote West Pokot. The court also charged Wandetto with publishing false news in connection with an article (date unavailable) in which he quoted a minister in President Moi's government who called for the posthumous trial of Jomo Kenyatta, the first president of Kenya, for alleged 'crimes' committed during his presidency. The minister denied calling for such a trial. The court granted bail on the fresh charge. (NDIMA)

On 29 February Royal Media, the parent company of Citizen Radio, lost its bid to have Telkon Kenya, the Communication Commission of Kenya (CCK) and Kenya Broadcasting Corporation (KBC) reconnect power to its transmitters in Londiani, Nyeri and Nyambene

(*Index* 2/2000). Justice Kassanga Mulwa struck out the application with costs, arguing that Royal Media had knowingly entered into an agreement with Telkom Kenya and that Citizen had transmitted when it was illegal to do so. However, on 1 March CCK was ordered to restore the frequencies it had withdrawn pending the hearing of an appeal. (NDIMA)

On 13 March **Simi Kusimba**, a *People Daily* journalist arrested on 11 March, was charged with publishing an alarmist article 'calculated to cause fear and alarm among the public' that political activist Omar Masumbuko had gone underground to avoid arrest after four policeman were caught in connection with the disappearance of a four-tonne hashish haul. Kusimba was released on bond. The story, initially denied by police, was covered by the Kenya Broadcasting Corporation, *Daily Nation*, the *Standard* and *Kenya Times* prompting police to reassure the public that the drug haul was intact. On 15 March **Sam Aola**, a correspondent for Agence-France Presse and the *People Daily*, was arrested and charged with putting out an 'alarmist report' related to the same drugs story. (Media Institute, RSF)

KUWAIT

On 26 March an appeals court upheld the convictions on short-story writer **Laila al-'Othman** (*Index* 2/2000)and **Dr 'Aliya Shu'ayb** (*Index* 2/2000), although the punishments were reduced. The court upheld the finding that al-'Othman's book, *The Departure*, was immoral, but the two-month prison sentence was dropped and instead al-'Othman and her publisher **Yahiya al-Rubay'an** were fined KD1,000 (US$3,260) each for 'immorality'. The court also overturned the two-month prison sentence against Shu'ayb for defaming religion and instead fined her and al-Rubay'an KD100 (US$326) each for publishing Shu'ayb's collection of poetry, *Spiders Bemoan a Wound*, without a permit. Both books were also banned, although publication and distribution of *The Departure* had been legal in Kuwait since 1984.

KYRGYZSTAN

TV journalist Erkin Turaliev told a press conference in Bishkek on 11 February that presidential press secretary Osmonarkun Ibraimov asked him to produce programmes slandering **Djypar Djeksheev** and **Feliks Kulov**, leaders of the Democratic Movement of Kyrgyzstan and the Ar-Namys Party respectively. Both parties were barred from contending the 20 February parliamentary election. Turaliev produced a recording of the telephone conversation in which Ibraimov made the request. (RFE/RL)

Roza Kachieva, founder of semi-private Shade TV, was charged with embezzlement on 21 March. Kachieva was detained in mid-January. She attributes her arrest to her stated intention to prepare a series of programmes on opposition politicians. (RFE/RL)

On 16 March officers from the ministry of internal affairs arrested *Res Publica* journalist **Aziza Abdrasulova** and

charged her with 'participating in an unsanctioned meeting'. Earlier that day, Abdrasulova had covered a peaceful rally in Bishkek to protest alleged fraud in the 12 March parliamentary run-off elections. Abdrasulova underwent a strip search, was detained without food or heat and denied the right to legal counsel. Following an all-night trial, during which she was also denied the right to defend herself, Abdrasulova was released on 18 March, after paying a fine of 1,000 soms (about US$20). On 27 March, the state legal lepartment ordered the Uchkon publishing company to cease printing *Res Publica* until the paper pays an earlier fine of 200,000 soms (US$4,200) for alleged slander. On 29 March, the Bishkek prosecutor's office reprimanded *Res Publica* editor **Zamira Sydykova** for publishing political leaflets to be handed out during protest rallies. On 31 March a Bishkek district court imposed a further 40,000 som (about US$850) fine on *Res Publica* for libel. The newspaper's chief editor and a journalist were fined 5,000 soms each. The concerted legal harassment that *Res Publica* has faced in recent months (*Index* 3/1999, 4/1999, 5/1999, 2/2000) has intensified as it has reported election irregularities. The local newspaper *Delo No* has also been threatened with suspension after publishing international criticisms of the election, while the opposition newspaper *Asab* was recently fined 2 million soms (US$42,000) for alleged tax code violations. (WAN, CPJ, RFE/RL)

Nigmatulla Bazakov, an outpoken leader of the 50,000-

strong Uighur minority, was shot dead outside his home in Bishkek on 28 March. One or more unknown assailants fired two shots at Bazakov's head at point-blank range. (RFE/RL, Reuters)

LAOS

Two correspondents of Australia's ABC network, **Ginny Stein** and **David Leland**, were arrested on 30 March in Vientiane while filming the debris of a restaurant that had been destroyed in a bomb attack. The journalists had official authorisation, but the authorities said they were 'not allowed to cover this event'. (RSF, CPJ)

LEBANON

On 17 March **Ramzi Haidar**, a photographer with Agence-France Presse, and **Hassan Mounla**, a photographer with Associated Press, were beaten with truncheons and their film was confiscated while covering a demonstration against the expulsion of four members of the Japanese Red Army. (RSF)

LIBERIA

President Charles Taylor has pulled all government advertising from independent newspapers and instructed the Bureau of General Auditing to audit the papers' finances, after describing the private media as 'anti-patriotic', it was reported on 24 March. The papers, including *The Inquirer* and *The News*, had denounced the closure on 15 March of independent radio stations Radio Veritas and Star Radio (*Index* 1/1999). The stations were closed down for 'inciting insecurity'. (PANA)

After intervention by the US ambassador, the government re-opened the Catholic-run Radio Veritas on 23 March. President Taylor said the station would be allowed to transmit as long as it reported solely on religious matters but that Star would never again broadcast while he remained in power. (BBC Online)

MALAYSIA

On 2 March Minister of Home Affairs Datuk Seri Ahmad Badawi told **Chia Lim Thye**, owner and publisher of the bi-weekly *Harakah* (*Index* 1/2000, 2/2000), that he was no longer authorised to publish twice a month and that, if he did not respect these conditions, the paper would be closed. Deputy Minister of Home Affairs Datuk Chor Chee Heung, originally said the new ruling applied also to the Internet edition of *Harakah* but, after a flurry of confusion, Chor reiterated the government's commitment to its stated policy of no Internet censorship. (RSF, WAN, *Far Eastern Economic Review*)

The Home Ministry confirmed on 25 March that the publishing permit of popular pro-*reformasi* magazine *Detik* will not be renewed. *Detik* has not been published since December when its permit was suspended along with three others (*Index* 2/2000). The newspapers *Al-Wasilah*, *Eksklusif* and *Tamadun* are still waiting for the renewal of their licences.(*Aliran*, CPJ)

MAURITANIA

Opposition weekly *L'Eveil Hebdo* has had its publishing licence revoked for one month, it was reported on 17 February. The authorities seized issue 332 of the paper in reaction to an article dealing with Islamic terrorist networks in the country. (RSF)

MEXICO

On 9 April border police discovered the body of **Pablo Pineda**, a reporter and photographer for *La Opinion* newspaper, on the US side of the Rio Grande near Harlingen, Texas. The agents observed two men on the Mexican side of the river dump a large package into the water: on inspection they discovered it contained Pineda's executed body, not drugs as they had suspected. (IPI)

On 2 March **Ángel Méndez**, correspondent with the dailies *Panorama* and *La Voz de Michoacán*, was taken to the police station at Coahuayana and interrogated about his sources. The same day the journalist had published information about clashes between the army and alleged factions of the Popular Revolutionary Army (EPR). Also on 2 March, the governor reportedly accused all journalists who print 'this kind of information' of being guilty of 'destabilising the state'. (RSF)

MOROCCO

The 4 March edition of the French daily *Le Figaro* was blocked from distribution for carrying an article based on the book *Secrets of the King's Friend*, written by the late King Hassan's personal doctor **François Cleret**. The article revealed that the rebel 'Mehdi Ben Barak's body was cut into pieces under orders of King Hasan and brought to Morocco in diplomatic suitcases'. On 15 February French weekly *Jeune Afrique-l'Intelligent* had been blocked from distribution because of an article by Moroccan exile **Abdellah Labdaoui**, which expressed serious doubts about the ability of the King Mohammed VI to effect real change and punish the abusers of human rights under his father's rule. (RSF)

The fourth edition of a new liberal political weekly remained stuck at the printers on 31 March due to non-payment of costs. Since its launch three weeks earlier *Demain* had come under intense pressure for touching on taboo issues, such as negotiations with the Polisario Liberation Front, Islamism and the presence of Mossad agents in Morocco. In the run-up to the fourth edition, government reportedly forced shareholders to sell their stocks to Abdennasser Bouzza, who is closely linked to the royal palace. On 30 March managing editor **Ali Lmrabet** told the press that Bouzza, with 72% of the shares, had insisted on his right to vet the contents before authorising funds to pay for printing. (RSF, CPJ)

MOZAMBIQUE

The independent fax newspaper *Metical* reported on 28 March that Maputo's Sunday *Domingo*, a paper privatised in 1983, had refused to publish a paid advertisement from striking lecturers at the Social Science Faculty (UFICS) at Eduardo Mondlane University. Initially *Domingo* accepted payment for the ad in its 26 March edition but it was spiked by the management. Instead *Domingo* carried an editorial saying that it refused to publish text 'that mixed together the visit of [East Timorese leader] Xanana Gusmao with the strike, and which complained of an authoritarian and repressive atmosphere at UFICS'. (MISA).

NAMIBIA

Black resident **Wayne Lindenberg** was detained by police for giving the 'thumbs down' sign to the passing motorcade of Prime Minister Hage Geingob on 7 March. Lindenberg said police officers physically and verbally abused him during his detention. He was released without charge but has since laid charges of assault. Geingob later issued a statement saying Lindenberg should not think he had the 'freedom to make obscene gestures'. (MISA)

NEPAL

On 26 February **Suresh Ale Magar**, a journalist with the daily *Janadesh*, was released from custody. He had been held for more than eight weeks at the army barracks in Pokhara, Kaski district, for having alleged ties with Maoist guerrillas. (RSF)

Jagdish Bhattarai, editor of the local weekly *Nava Chetna* and correspondent for *Kantipur Daily* in Palpa and the *Kathmandu Post*, was sentenced to seven days in jail and fined 500 rupees (approx. US$7.20) for contempt of court on 12 March. The case arose because of an editorial he published on 12 December 1998 under the headline 'When defenders of the law become corrupt', which denounced favours in the legal system. (CPJ, RSF)

Recent Publication: *Nepal: Human Rights and Security* (AI, February 2000, pp 17).

NIGERIA

A man accused of drinking alcohol in public has become the first person sentenced under *sharia* law in the northern state of Zamfara. It was reported on 21 February that about 500 people watched as **Bashiri Sule** received 80 lashes near the emir's palace in Gusau (*West Africa*).

Twelve armed security men stormed the publishing offices of the *Nigerian Tribune*, shutting down the premises on 2 March. The security agents' leader told the newspaper's workers that the president's office had ordered them to stop distribution of that day's edition. (Independent Journalism Centre)

Security forces swooped on newspaper stands in Bayela state on 9 March, removing copies of *Banner News* and *Independent Monitor. Banner News'* publisher **Union Oyadongha** was also arrested and detained. In a report yet to be confirmed, Oyadongha was released from jail a week later. The operation was reportedly connected to articles published in both newspapers on the widespread sectarian violence that has erupted since the adoption of *sharia* law in some provinces. (Independent Journalism Centre, CPJ)

Nine armed State Security Service (SSS) officers blocked off the offices of *This Day* newspaper for three hours on 4 April, abusing staff members and accusing them of harbouring 'subversive and incriminating

documents'. The SSS later explained to reporters that their officers had intended to arrest editor-in-chief **Nduaka Obiagbena** in connection with an unpaid hotel bill of US$24,000 run up in Washington in September while covering the IMF/World Bank meeting. Obiagbena resigned from his editorial position on 7 April. (Independent Journalism Centre, PANA)

PAKISTAN

On 25 February Justice Rehmat Hussain Jafri decided to censor all media coverage of the trial of former prime minister Nawaz Sharif and six others for hijacking, attempted murder and terrorism. The prosecution submitted its application to restrict media coverage on 23 February on the grounds that statements made by the defendants are 'likely to tarnish and affect the security, integrity and solidarity of the Islamic republic of Pakistan'. (CPJ)

Iqbal Raad, one of the principal lawyers defending Nawaz Sharif, was assassinated in his Karachi office along with two other people on 10 March. (*International Herald Tribune*)

PALESTINE AUTHORITY

On 18 February **Dr Abdul al-Sattar Qassim** (*Index 2/2000*), one of the signatories of a document calling for an end to corruption, was re-arrested at his home in Nablus on the orders of Police Chief Major General Ghazi Jabali and Yasser Arafat himself. Dr Qassim's wife said the rearresting officers had no warrant and told her they 'needed him for questioning for only 15 minutes'. (LAW, Network of Concerned Historians)

It was reported on 22 February that Hebron Police Chief Tariq Zeid ordered the immediate closure of Nawras TV for airing interviews with striking teachers. (Palestine Human Rights Monitoring Group)

On 29 February PA Police Chief Jabali announced a ban on all public demonstrations, probably to prevent a mass rally planned in Ramallah to show solidarity with at least 35 detained Bir Zeit University students. Following uproar at French Foreign Minister Lionel Jospin's comment that Lebanese resistance to Israeli occupation was 'terrorism', police cracked down on dissenting students, who were taken to intelligence headquarters at Jericho where they were allegedly subjected to torture. (LAW, Human Rights Action Project, *Hanthala*)

On 22 March a crew from the French television station France 2 was 'taken to task' by police at the south entrance to Bethlehem, which was then welcoming Pope John Paul II. They forbade the crew from filming, confiscated a cassette and searched the vehicle for other cassettes. (RSF)

Khaled Amaryeh, editor-in-chief of the new Hebron bi-monthly *Akhbar al-Khalil* (Hebron Times), was summoned by PA General Intelligence officers on 11 February to a 'meeting' where he was questioned on an editorial on the Palestinian refugees' right of return. Amaryeh says he was accused of 'doubting the state's

commitment to the refugees' cause and of inciting the refugees against the leadership'. On 15 February he was summoned by an Israeli District Coordination Office official and questioned on the same issue, and warned against 'incitement'. (OMCT, Palestine Human Rights Monitoring Group)

PERU

Journalist **Juan Ramírez Vásquez**, head of local television programme *Hechos* (Facts) in Pucallpa, Ucayali district, sought the protection of the authorities on 1 February after receiving a letter warning of a plot to assassinate him. (IPYS)

Fernando Alfaro Venturo, director and host of political analysis TV programme *Línea de Mira* (Line of Vision) broadcast by Canal 6 in Pucallpa, Ucayali district, claimed that reruns of his weekly show were stopped on 8 February because of coverage he gave to cases of censorship at the TV station. (IPYS)

For the second time in two weeks, Lima-based radio station Radio 1160 was forced to stop broadcasting on 2 February after its sound equipment and transmitter were seized by authorities. Although the court order was given in connection with a pending debt by the station, Radio 1160's owners claim the seizure was a political move to silence a programme by journalist **César Hildebrandt**, an outspoken critic of corruption in President Alberto Fujimori's government (*Index* 2/1998, 4/1998, 4/1999, 6/1999, 2/2000). Four days before the seizure, Hildebrandt had gone on

air with his *Ondas de Libertad* (Waves of Freedom) programme to interview Fujimori's ex-wife, Susana Higuchi. (IFJ)

The offices of Canal 10 television station in Huaral, north of Lima, were broken into on 7 February by unknown assailants who stole expensive broadcast equipment, cash and tax payment receipts. The break-in happened on the eve of the station's relaunch of investigative current affairs programme *Contacto Directo* (Direct Contact). (IFJ)

Press photographers **José Abanto** and **Jhony Laurente**, of Lima daily *La República*, were beaten and had had their cameras destroyed on 22 February by two assailants while investigating pro-President Alberto Fujimori election T-shirts allegedly being produced with government funds. The incident occurred 24 hours after the Public Prosecutor's Office ordered a follow-up into a report in *La República* giving evidence of the alleged contracting of garment factories, trucks and personnel by the National Intelligence Service to support President Fujimori's electoral campaign. (IPYS)

Teobaldo Menéndez Fachín, director and host of radio programme *Inédito* in Yurimaguas, Loreto, was beaten and threatened with death on 26 February by two unidentified attackers who criticised the anti-government content of his broadcasts. (IPYS)

Lima daily *La República* reporter **Ana María Tejada Purizaca** was allegedly kidnapped and had an interview recording destroyed on 1 March by Walter Chipoco

Espinoza, the electoral campaign manager of ruling party congresswoman, Carmen Lozada de Gamboa. (IFJ)

Press photographer **Edwin Anyosa** of daily *La Voz de Ica* suffered a broken nose and lost his camera after allegedly being attacked on 2 March by municipal worker José Vera Mendoza during a violent demonstration by striking local-government employees in Ica. (IFJ)

A bomb planted by three hooded assailants went off in the premises of Radio Junín, in Junín province, on 5 March. According to Radio Junín manager **Jacinto Figueroa Yauri**, the station started receiving threatening phone calls after a report critical of the government was broadcast on 23 February on its news programme *Las Noticias en Radio Junín*. (IFJ)

Lima daily *El Comercio* is facing charges of fraud and bribery in what is seen as a ploy by a minority of pro-government shareholders to take control of the paper – Peru's oldest and most respected. *El Comercio's* former general manager, Luís García Miró, went on television on 12 March to announce that he was suing the paper for US$20 million for allegedly forcing him to sell his shares in the business six years ago and cheating him of his redundancy payment. A few days later, an investigation was launched into the paper's possible involvement in a dollar scam at Peru's Exchange Rate Market. García's attack followed a controversial exposé published by *El Comercio* on 29 February accusing ruling party members of forging the one million signatures

needed to register Fujimori as an electoral candidate. (IFJ, CPJ, RSF)

Journalist **Luis Ugaz Espinoza**, presenter of local radio programme *Yo soy la voz del Pueblo* in Iquitos province, was physically assaulted and threatened with death on 14 March by two unidentified individuals who broke into his studio while he was on the air. (IPYS)

The presses of two opposition Lima dailies were seized two days before the general election on 9 April. The seizure was ordered by Lima's 59th civil court in connection with an unpaid debt of US$260,000 owed by the owner of printing company LEA S.A. *Punto Final* editor **Francisco Loayza Galván** claimed the seizure order was a ploy by the government to gag two independent papers opposed to President Alberto Fujimori's regime. (IFJ)

In the first half of March, Radio Huascarán news bulletin editor **Gerardo Rocha Chacos**, and daily *La Jornada* editor **Edgar Palma Huerta**, were sacked by their bosses for reports criticising high-ranking government officials. **Robin Hood Ipanaqué Hidalgo** was also pushed out after his radio news programme *La Noticia*, broadcast on Radio Visión Alegría, was pulled by the owners for regularly criticising regional government officials. In early April, **Alberto Ramos Romero**, editor of Radio Ancash's news programme in Huaraz, was forced to resign after a 26 March broadcast in which he criticised President Alberto Fujimori's government.

Seven people were injured when a home-made bomb exploded outside DXMS, a Roman Catholic radio station in the southern island of Mindanao on 27 February. The attack took place just before the start of a regular programme by broadcaster **Zamzamin Ampatuan**, who has blamed Muslim separatists for a ferry bombing and two bus explosions that killed at least 45 people. A second assassination attempt took place on 27 March when 14 men attacked Ampatuan killing one of his body guards and injuring five others. Ampatuan was wounded. Police suspect Jack Abdullah, alias Commander Putao, of Moro Islamic Liberation Front as being responsible for the latest attack. (WAN, CPJ, RSF, CMFR)

First Deputy Media Minister Mikhail Seslavinskii warned journalists on 14 March that any press or television interview with Chechen President Aslan Maskhadov, Field Commander Shamil Basaaev or former Foreign Minister Movladi Udugov will be considered a violation of the Russian law on combating terrorism. (RFE/RL)

The head of information at the Justice Commission, Andrei Morozov, said on 24 February that the government's commission on Operational Issues would examine legislation on information security on 28 March, two days after presidential elections. He said that 'everything that is distributed on the Internet would be placed on the same footing as a document that should be examined in court.' (RFE/RL)

Media Minister Mikhail Lesin announced on 29 February that the licences of Russian Public Television (ORT) and TV-Tsentr would not automatically be renewed because of their 'slanted coverage' of the lead-up to the 19 December State duma elections. He added that this was not a political decision but was based more upon pure 'technicality' as channels that have received official warnings are not automatically granted licence renewals. (RFE/RL)

The Primore regional court has overturned a ruling by a Vladistock court and ordered the head of Federal Security Service's Pacific Fleet directorate, **Nikolai Sotskov**, to pay the sum of 25,000 rubles (approx. US$875) in damages to environmentalist **Grigorii Pasko** (*Index* 1/1997, 2/1999, 3/1999, 5/1999). Pasko, who was arrested in November 1997 on suspicion of revealing classified information about the Pacific Fleet's hazardous treatment of nuclear waste, was found guilty in July 1999 of abuse of office. (RFE/RL)

The interior ministry announced on 16 February that it would drop the case against *Moskovskii komsomolets* reporter **Aleksandr Khinshteyn**, who was accused in January of 'concealing a psychiatric disorder' when he applied for a driver's licence (*Index* 2/2000). His newspaper believes the case was manufactured by the ministry to pressure him into ending his investigative pieces about 'oligarch' Boris Berezovskii and other figures. (RFE/RL)

A spokesman for the Primorskii Krai directorate of the FSB announced on 21 February that environmental researcher **Valerii Soifer** had been found with documents that could be of use to NATO. Soifer had his home and laboratory raided by FSB agents in July 1999, and was accused of misusing classified documents in his research on the ecological effects of a nuclear submarine accident in 1985. In February a court in Vladistock ordered the FBS to return some of the material confiscated during the raid. Another environmental researcher, **Igor Sutyagin**, remains imprisoned in Kaluga Oblast as investigators there try to prove that he is a spy. (RFE/RL)

SERBIA-MONTENEGRO

Halil Matoshi, an Albanian journalist with the Albanian-language newspaper Zeri, was released from prison in Pozarevac on 28 January. He had been held in prison without charge since June 1999. (ANEM)

The host of Pink TV, **Milovan 'Minimaks' Ilic**, was taken off air by management on 27 February and had his contract suspended. The suspension came after the band Indeksovo Pozoriste appeared on his show in a clip that contained a lyric referring to police violence against demonstrators and the misery of the Serbian people. The programme reached a record-breaking 20 million viewers. (ANEM)

Dissident artist **Bogoljub 'Maki' Arsenijevic** escaped from custody in a Belgrade hospital on 8 March by climbing down a lightning rod from the third-floor window of the clinic where he was being held. He was jailed for three years after initiating civilian protests in the central Serbian city of Valjevo. (Free B92)

Seven student activists, a photographer from the Belgrade daily *Glas javnosti* and a Montenegrin television cameraman, **Bojan Erdeljanovic**, were detained by Novi Sad police on 17 March during a protest by the Novi Sad branch of the student movement Otpor. Police claimed the arrests were made because the protest was not registered. All nine were released. (ANEM)

Nebojsa Ristic, editor-in-chief of Sokobanja's TV Soko, was released on 17 March from Zajecar prison after serving more than 11 months of a one-year prison term. Ristic was convicted last April of 'disseminating false information' for having displayed the Radio B92 poster 'Free Press, Made in Serbia' in his office. (ANEM)

SOMALIA

On 26 February **Ahmed Kafi Awale**, a commentator with Radio of Somali People, was shot dead by thieves while reporting from Mogadishu's Bakara market. Three others were killed and seven were injured. Radio of the Somali People is controlled by the Mogadishu warlord Hussein Mohamed Aidid. Awale is the first Somali journalist killed in the course of duty since the death of **Mohamed Abdi Afgoye** of Radio Mogadishu in a 1993 attack by UN peacekeepers. (RSF)

Journalist **Mohamed Salad Ali**,

ANDREY BABITSKY
Upfront

Naum Nim: The authorities are trying to impress on us the idea that journalists are, above all, citizens. A journalist is not there to do a job, but to 'take part in the information war'. Do journalists in war have obligations beyond a responsibility to their editors?

Andrey Babitsky: I come down on on the side of journalism with a moral orientation. Anyone who comes face to face with poverty, grief or crime evaluates the experience in some way and, if he talks or writes about it, his judgment will be expressed in the composition, the shape of his writing. Journalists love to say they are simply witnesses to events. This isn't true. The best form of journalism is reportage. I have never thought of myself as a journalist, I try to work on the periphery. In my view, journalism is closely related to literature. It has a multi-genre quality which links it to academic disciplines: philosophy, history or sociology.

The legacy and values of Christian civilisation are vital. I can't understand how one can avoid or ignore them, and turn journalistic writing into dry reporting analogous to the statement of a witness in court. Journalistic responsibility is a serious issue. I thought about it when I was waiting to be killed. It seemed to me then that the situation I had found myself in was a kind of retribution – yes – a descent into the abyss, into fear, the crumbling of personal dignity. I was very broken psychologically, but there was also a deep space which remained untouched throughout.

I'd taken the deaths I saw too lightly. Soldiers and officers corpses. This has to be published, don't cut it. We turned the bodies over so that it would be easier to photograph them. We didn't treat them in the way Christian believers should, we didn't act like people for whom the mystery of death really exists. But this is the misfortune of humanity at war: it isn't confined to journalists. The logic of war is madness. Like a soldier, a journalist needs to be morally and psychologically rehabilitated after living in these conditions. I'm not justifying myself. I think guilt is guilt, even if it can be explained. The value of human life in war is as negligible for a reporter as it is for a soldier.

I have this dialogue with myself and my conscience constantly now. I don't understand it all myself yet. I feel at fault before everyone who wants to know the truth about what is happening. So many people have been denied access to the material I wrote about the war. My own words became an insurmountable obstacle. People couldn't read what I had written. I stand guilty before them and before those about whom I was writing, because my reporting did not get

● ●

to the audience at which it was directed.

My own perception of Russia's future is very different from that of the authorities. I have children, a wife, I have my friends. I believe that my country's future is my business and the business of every person living in it. My own ideas shouldn't necessarily have to conform to those of the government. The authorities shouldn't in any case be formulating an ideological doctrine for the development of the country. Government should be free of ideology. The image of the Russian people is not a matter for the authorities, it is an issue for Russians themselves and for their national culture.

Russia will have a dictatorship which could be either benign or harsh. It's more likely to be harsh if you consider that Putin favours the kind of military and police rule that is being enforced in Chechnya. Control will be established in areas indispensable to the government. For example, the country will no longer be sucked dry by oligarchs. They will simply come under the control of the centre and the entire criminal operation with be concentrated in a single pair of hands. It also seems to me that the principles of the market economy will remain virtually untouched. I'm even prepared to speculate that, in order to have good relations with the West, Putin will try to demonstrate that freedom of the press does exist and that some central publications will be obliged to play the role of 'opposition' media. But the provincial press is likely to be smothered by local authorities. Putin needs the provinces – that is where the iron hand will descend – he doesn't need Moscow as much.

The present regime has no conception of the value of human life. These are people who came to power on the crest of a very muddy wave. For the moment they are still a bunch of backstreet thugs, none too clean but teachable – you can see that by looking at Putin. The Putin of a month ago and Putin today are two quite different people. His language is clearer, he is learning, his phraseology is beginning to look more 'democratic'. But this regime has no notion of inalienable rights and freedoms, nor of the inviolability of freedom of speech. They will try to ape things, though, even if they don't understand that inalienable values do exist. ❑

Andrey Babitsky, a journalist with RFE/RL, disappeared in Chechnya on 20 January (Index 2/00). He was released by the Russian authorities on 29 February. Interview by Naum Nim, editor of Dos'e na Tzensuru. See also p172 Translated by Irena Maryniak

● ●

with the private daily *Qaran*, was arrested on 14 March and taken to the Hariryale Islamic court jail in Mogadishu. The arrest was in connection with articles on the same day in which prominent people denounced businessmen illegally trading in charcoal to the United Arab Emirates. The articles accused them of deforesting Somalia. (RSF)

SRI LANKA

On 1 February President Kumaratunga's cabinet re-activated several colonial era regulations set out in the Establishment Code (EC) that 'guide' the conduct of public officials. According to a proposal by Media Minister Mangala Samaraweera, public officials will be prohibited from giving interviews, criticising government actions or acting as whistle-blowers for stories in the public interest. (Free Media Movement)

On 3 April a grenade was thrown at the house of journalist **Nellai G. Nadesan**, the Batticaloa correspondent for the Tamil-language daily *Virakesarai*. Nadesan was not injured. (RSF)

Recent Publications: *Post-colonial Insecurities: India, Sri Lanka and the Question of Nationhood* by Sankaran Krishna (University of Minnesota Press, 1999, pp 316); *Sri Lankan Tamil Nationalism: Its Origins and Development in the 19th and 20th Centuries* by A. Jeyaratnam Wilson (Hurst & Co., 1999, pp 203)

SUDAN

Five journalists from the independent daily *As-Sahafa* and a

poet were detained in Khartoum on 24 March in connection with articles and poems deemed to have an anti-government slant. The move followed publication of articles by opponents of the regime. The editor-in-chief, **Kamal Hassan Bekheit**, editor **Ahmed Oumerabi**, and journalists **Abdel Kader Hafez**, **Rebei Hamid** and **Anwar al-Tikraina** were released just after midnight after signing an undertaking to report for further interrogation. The poet remains unidentified. (Agence-France Presse)

SWAZILAND

The offices of the state-owned *Swazi Observer* were forced to close on 17 March, following a four-month-long campaign by government and police to persuade staff to identify the source of a leaked letter written by Police Commissioner Edgar Hillary. (CPJ)

On 23 March Swaziland Television Broadcasting Corporation fired 31 employees at the centre of a wage-related strike last year. The workers took control of the station studios on 28 October 1999 to demand a seven per cent payment of wages owing. The board made the sackings despite an inquiry which determined the strike was not illegal. (MISA)

TANZANIA

On 10 February the Zanzibar authorities threatened legal action against Press Services' **Mwinyio Sadallah** whose article in the Kiswahili paper *Nipashe* one week earlier claimed that the government was preparing to

publish a bill allowing President Salmin Amour to run for a third term. According to Television Zanzibar, Zanzibar Information Services had given Sadallah seven days to apologise. Sadallah, however, stood by his account of events. (MISA)

On 2 March editor of the Kiswahili daily *Kisheshe* **Vanance Mlay** was interrogated following his arrest for publishing a story on 18 January that alleged that Mbeya police had shot a Tunduma resident to death following a pursuit. The police consider the story seditious. Mlay was held in detention for five hours before being released on bail. (MISA)

TUNISIA

Civil rights activist and journalist **Taoufik Ben Brick** began a hunger strike on 3 April in protest at the interior ministry's refusal to return his passport confiscated in April 1999 (*Index* 4/99). On 10 April he was forcibly evicted from the premises of the Editions Aloe publishing house and brought before the magistrate. A correspondent with Reporters sans frontières, the French daily *La Croix* and the Infosud and Syfia press agencies, Ben Brick is charged with 'publishing false information' as a result of articles published in two foreign publications. The first, a book review of *Our Friend Ben Ali* by French journalists **Jean-Pierre Touquoi** and **Nicholas Beau**, appeared in the Swiss daily *Le Courrier*, while a second Swiss daily *Le Temps* exposed the political harassment of publisher **Sihem Ben Sedrine**, owner of Editions Aloe (*Index* 2/2000). (HRW, RSF, CPJ)

TURKEY

The *Chronological Album of The Kurds: 1900 to 2000*, a book distributed by the pro-Kurdish daily *Ozgur Bakis* (*Index* 5/1999, 1/2000), was banned on 5 February on the grounds it is 'separatist propaganda'. (Kurdish Observer, *Ozgur Bakis*)

The one-year-old, pro-Kurdish review *Serbesti* has had its sixth issue confiscated, it was reported on 9 February. Editor-in-chief **Ahmet Zeki Okçuoglu** (*Index* 3/1999), a former lawyer of imprisoned Kurdish Workers Party leader Abdullah Öcalan, claimed the ban was an indication of the authorities' reluctance to implement the reform promised after last year's Amnesty Law came into effect. The editor faces a 15-year prison sentence for comments he allegedly made on the now-defunct Kurdish channel, Med-TV, about Öcalan's trial for treason (*Index* 5/1996, 2/1997, 5/1997, 2/1998, 6/1998, 1/1999). (*Cildekt*, Kurdistan Observer)

RTUK, the Supreme Board of Television and Radio, ordered CNN-Turk off the air for one day, it was reported on 18 February, after the new 24-hour channel broadcast a programme on 13 January about the commuted death sentence on Abdullah Öcalan. 'Of course we are going to court,' said CNN-Turk presenter **Mehmet Ali Birand** (*Index* 4/1998). 'We are not going to let them get away with this.' (Associated Press, *Turkish Daily News*)

On 24 February the president of the legal Kurdish party (HADEP) **Ahmet Turan Demir**, and his predecessor **Murat Bozlak** (*Index* 1/1999, 5/1999), as well as 16 other party members were each sentenced to three years and nine months' imprisonment for 'supporting and receiving' on behalf of the PKK. A few hours earlier, a court in the south-east charged and jailed three local mayors on similar charges. **Feridun Celik**, **Feyzullah Karasalan** and **Selim Özalp** had been elected at last year's local council elections. The prosecution's file contained 400 pages of details of 'log-ons' made from municipality computers to the Internet sites of two Kurdish newspapers, *Ozgur Bakis* and *Ozgur Politika*. (*Cildekt*)

On 29 February security police arrested *Ozgur Bakis* reporter **Numan Altinas**, who was on assignment reporting the protests surrounding the detentions of the HADEP mayors. (Kurdish Observer)

Lawyer and writer **Esber Yagmurdereli** (*Index* 2/1998, 4/1998, 6/1999), jailed for 25 years for criticising Turkey's treatment of its Kurds, won France's Ludovic Trarieux prize for defending human rights, it was reported on 7 March. The writer has been in jail since June 1998 for a speech proposing a peaceful solution to the Kurdish problem. (Agence-France Presse, Kurdistan Observer)

Seven officials of the Labour Party were each sentenced to six months in prison by a court in Elazig for singing songs in Kurdish last May, it was reported on 8 March. (Evrensel)

Kurdish poet **Yilmaz Odabasi** (*Index* 6/1999), released last year under the new Amnesty Law, returned to prison on 8 March on charges of 'insulting the court'. At his original hearing Odabasi had protested his sentence, saying 'I am ashamed of living in the same age and the same country as you'. (PEN)

Award-winning singer **Ahmet Kaya** (*Index* 5/1999) was sentenced *in absentia* to 45 months in prison for singing in front of a picture of Abdullah Öcalan in Berlin in 1993, it was reported on 10 March. Kaya, who was abroad during the trial, said he would not return 'under these circumstances'. (Agence-France Presse, Kurdistan Observer)

Former Prime Minister **Necmettin Erbakan** (*Index* 1/1998, 2/1998) was sentenced on 11 March to a year in prison for a speech in 1994 in which he asserted that Turkey had drifted away from its Islamic roots, and that secular politicians had driven a wedge between ethnic Kurds and other citizens. (*New York Times*, Kurdistan Observer)

On 17 March the European Court of Human Rights ruled that Turkey had violated 'the right to free expression' by suppression of the pro-Kurdish newspaper, *Ozgur Gundem* (*Index* 2/1995 3/1995, 5/1995). Another ruling on 29 March found that Turkey had failed to protect the life of *Ozgur Gundem* journalist, **Kemal Kilic**, who was shot dead by unknown perpetrators after months of harassment and attacks at the bureau in Sanliurfa. (KHRP)

Two *imams*, **Muhyeddin Karaalp** and **Adil Kahraman**,

who gave sermons in Kurdish at Halidye Mosque in Antalya, were taken to the Security Directorate by plain-clothes policemen, it was reported on 28 March. They explained that their congregations could neither speak nor understand Turkish. (Kurdish Observer)

Akin Birdal (*Index* 4/1998, 5/1998, 1/1999, 4/1999, 5/1999, 6/1999, 1/2000, 2/2000), former president of the Turkish Human Rights Association and Vice-President of the International Human Rights Federation (FIHD), returned to prison on 28 March to serve the remainder of his one-year sentence for 'racial provocation'. The Turkish courts rejected a medical report certifying that he was unfit to return to prison because of the injuries he received in the assassination attempt on him in 1998. (AI, *Cildekt*, Kurdish Observer)

All of Kurdish writer **Mehmet Uzun**'s books were confiscated in police raids on bookshops on 30 March. They told booksellers they were implementing a 4 February decision of the Diyarbakir security court. Uzun is based in Sweden, where he fled in 1977 after being imprisoned and tortured by the authorities. (Norwegian Forum for Free Expression)

TURKMENISTAN

On 25 February a Turkmen district court sentenced **Nurberdy Nurmamedov**, leader of the unregistered Agzybirlik opposition movement, to five years in prison on charges of hooliganism and intent to commit murder (*Index* 2/2000).

Nurmamedov's son **Murad** was sentenced to two years in prison on charges of hooliganism. Foreign diplomats were barred from the court proceedings. (RFE/RL)

In early March the authorities arrested a young Baptist, **Chariyar Atakov**, whose brother **Shagildy Atakov** is serving a four-year sentence in a labour camp (*Index* 2/2000). (Keston News Service)

Between 11 and 13 March, the government deported to Russia three Baptist preachers and their families who had been living in Ashgabat and the south-eastern town of Mary (*Index* 2/2000). (Keston News Service)

Recent publication: *Harassment and Imprisonment of Religious Believers* (AI, March 2000, 14pp)

UKRAINE

Oleg Liachko, the editor-in-chief of the independent weekly *Svoboda* (Freedom), was attacked and beaten by two unidentified persons in the stairwell of his residence in Kiev. He had received threatening phone calls after the publication of a number of articles on 1 March which were critical of the secret service. Liachko was formally the editor-in-chief of the independent weekly *Politika*, which was found guilty in June 1999 of disclosing state secrets following the publication of articles about naval espionage. (RSF)

URUGUAY

Julio C De La Rosa, news director and owner of radio station CV 149 Radio del Centro

in the northern town of Baltasar Brum, was shot dead on 24 February by a former public official angered by comments in one of his broadcasts. Nery Colombo, who resigned from public office after an investigation into allegations of misconduct, stormed into De La Rosa's office, shot him and then shot himself, claiming that the broadcast had ruined his political career. (IAPA)

UK

London's Metropolitan Police, taken to court by the Free Tibet campaign, admitted in an out-of-court settlement on 3 May that 'it was unlawful for individual officers to remove banners and flags from people ... protesting against the Chinese regime' and that 'it would be unlawful to position police vans in front of protestors ... to suppress free speech'. The Free Tibet campaign took legal action following the suppression of protest during Chinese president Jiang Zemin's visit to London in October 1999 (*Index* 1/00).

The Scottish executive tried to end the controversy on the repeal of Section 28, which forbids the promotion of homosexuality in schools, by announcing on 25 February it will be replaced by a new clause stressing the importance of family values. Cardinal Thomas Winning, leader of Scotland's Roman Catholics, argued that the new clause was more likely to increase, rather than allay, concerns. (*Guardian*)

The government announced on 26 February that it intended to sue former MI5 agent **David Shayler** and the newspapers which published his allegations about the security services. The government wants to reclaim what it says are Shayler's profits from selling secrets. It claims that Shayler had breached his contract, the confidence of his employers and infringed Crown Copyright on the information to which he had access. In a related development mature student **Julie-Ann Davies** was arrested during a lecture at Kingston University on 6 March in connection with the Official Secrets Act. She is understood to been active in the campaign to get charges dropped against Shayler, whom she met while working as a researcher at Channel 4. (*Guardian, The Times, Daily Telegraph*)

It was reported on 7 March that the prime minister's wife, Cherie Blair, had began legal proceedings against the *Mail on Sunday,* her former nanny **Ros Mark** and her literary agent regarding an article in early editions about Mark's time at Downing Street. Both the newspaper and Mark could have been liable if it was proved that she they had knowingly breached the confidentiality agreement which she signed while working for the Blairs in 1997. After gaining an injunction, the Blairs said they believed that Mark was 'basically a good person' who had not intended to cause any harm. Mrs Blair and Mark issued a joint statement saying that no further legal action would be taken when all copies of the manuscript and a computer disk holding additional information were handed over. (*Guardian, The Times, Daily Telegraph*)

A Scottish judge ruled on 8 March that the trial of those accused of the Lockerbie bombing could not be televised by network television. The trial, due to start on 3 May, will be televised by closed circuit TV to victims' relatives but Lord MacFadyen ruled that a wider TV screening might intimidate the witnesses and prejudice proceedings. (*Guardian*)

The use of Public Immunity Certificates (PIC) to block evidence in criminal trials is likely to come under renewed scrutiny following judgements by the European Court of Human Rights (ECHR) on 10 March. PICs are used to block the release of information to the defence on public interest grounds. The ECHR recommended proper legal controls over use of the certificates. Once the Human Rights Act comes into force the issue is likely to be challenged in the British court system. (*Financial Times*)

The London office of the EU condemned the 'paranoid, sensationalist and ill-informed reporting of European issues in the British press' on 12 April. It accused newspapers of distorting coverage of Europe in the last few months, singling out the *Daily Mail* and *Sunday Telegraph* for particular criticism. (*Daily Telegraph*)

On 12 April David Irving, the controversial right-wing historian, lost his libel action against **Prof Deborah Lipstadt** and Penguin Books over claims that he was a 'Holocaust-denier'. The allegations were contained in Lipstadt's book *Denying the Holocaust.* Mr Justice Gray, in summing up, said that Irving had, for his own reasons, 'persistently and deliberately misrepresented and manipulated historical evidence'. (*Financial Times*)

USA

It was reported in February that, during the final days of the Kosovo war, several officers from the US Army's 4th Psychological Operations (PSYOPS) group worked in CNN's news division at the station's headquarters in Atlanta. In the 1980s, the group was involved in an agency which planted stories in the US media supporting the Reagan administration's Central American policies. The story has been ignored by the mainstream US media.(*Trouw, Intelligence Newsletter*)

On 25 February it was reported that in the first vote of its kind, the people of Holland, Michigan, had voted by a majority of 55% to 45% not to force their public library to filter access to the Internet on its public computers. (*New York Times Service*)

Tim Crews, a journalist with the *Sacremento Valley Mirror*, was given a five-day jail sentence for refusing to hand over the name of a confidential source to police. Crews was called 'obstinate and wrong-headed' by the judge, it was reported on 3 March, after he refused to reveal who told him that a police officer had stolen a handgun from a police anti-drug squad. (RSF)

US homosexuals have threatened to take nationwide action against Paramount, the film and television company, because it has given a TV show to a radio star who calls homosexuality 'deviant' and a 'biological error'. It was reported on 23 March that **Dr Laura Schlessinger** would take her three-hour daily talk show, which attracts 20 million listeners, on to television. Her critics know her as the 'Queen of Hate Radio' for her trenchant responses to listeners' calls. (*Daily Telegraph*)

Journalist **Errol Maitland** of radio WBAI was attacked on 25 March by members of the New York Police Department (NYPD) while covering the funeral of a Haitian-American Patrick Daismond, who was shot dead by an NYPD officer on 16 March. Maitland, 48, was thrown to the ground and arrested for disorderly conduct after providing live coverage of the funeral over his mobile phone. According to a witness, Maitland was 'trying to keep some distance from the cops' while filing his report. He was initially denied medical treatment in spite of complaining of widespread pain in his body and later that day, following a visit from his attorney, he was taken to hospital and placed in the coronary intensive care unit. (RSF*)*

It was reported on 27 March that Mattel, the company behind Internet filter software Cyberpatrol, has taken legal action against two cryptoanalysts who had published instructions on how to decipher the encrypted list of websites and newsgroups blocked by the filter. The attorney representing Cyberpatrol, Irwin Schwartz, was condemned the previous week by the American Civil Liberties Union (ACLU) for sending e-mails to the sites which either hosted, or wanted to, host the offending program, requesting

the identity of anyone who had downloaded it. (*Wired News*)

UZBEKISTAN

US State Department envoy John Beyrle told officials in Tashkent on 16 February that they should modify or replace the law on religion, which he described as one of the harshest in the world. (RFE/RL)

The World Association of Newspapers and the Committee to Protect Journalists renewed efforts in February and March to press for the release of radio journalist **Shadi Mardiyev**, who has spent three years in jail after being convicted of defaming a local prosecutor (*Index* 5/1998, 6/1998, 2/2000). Mardiyev's health is reportedly failing. (RFE/RL)

On 7 March police confiscated documents from a Human Rights Watch representative monitoring the trial at the Syrdarya district court of 12 men accused of membership in the banned Muslim organisation Hizb-ut-Takhrir. The confiscated material consisted of six copies of the Uzbekistan chapter of the HRW World Report, the organisation's annual global survey of human rights conditions. (RFE/RL, HRW)

Recent publications: *Makhbuba Kasymova and Ismail Adylov: Human Rights Defenders and Prisoners of Conscience* (AI, February 2000, 6pp and 7pp); *Leaving No Witnesses: Uzbekistan's Campaign Against Rights Defenders* (HRW, March 2000, 32pp)

VENEZUELA

Monthly *Exceso* reporter **Faitha Nahmens** and editor **Ben Ami Fihman** have gone into hiding after a Caracas judge ordered their arrest on 9 February for disobeying a summons to answer libel charges they claim are no longer legally valid. The charges date back to 1996, when the daughter of murdered businessman Casto Martínez sued *Exceso* for an article on the circumstances surrounding Martínez's shooting by paid assassins. Currently exiled in Paris, Fihman claims that the charges should have been dropped in February last year under statute of limitation rules. (RSF, *El País*)

In a televised address in March, President Hugo Chávez called reporters 'professional deceivers' and urged Venezuelans to 'unchain themselves from the dictatorship they represent'. On another occasion he warned: 'If they attack me, let them watch out, they'll get as good as they give.' (IAPA, CNN)

ZAMBIA

Journalists from four independent media organisations were barred from attending a public meeting between President Frederick Chiluba and his Malawi counterpart Bakili Muluzi on 10 March. The official news service, Zambia Information Services, revoked the invitations of journalists from *National Mirror*, Radio Phoenix, the *Monitor* and the *Post*, telling journalists there were insufficient places for all the media to attend. (MISA)

Independent journalist **Dickson**

Jere has been the target of threatening phone calls following the publication of an article which alleged the secret police breached UN sanctions against UNITA rebels in Angola. Jere, whose article was published in the *Monitor* on 24 March, says he received calls from three different men between 1 and 3 April warning him to 'lay off the story... or suffer severe repercussions'. Jere's story was based on a UN report which named the head of the secret service, Xavier Chungu, as a central figure in negotiations with UNITA. The report said Chungu was known to have had frequent meetings with a rebel involved in illegal diamond trading. (MISA)

ZIMBABWE

The Media Monitoring Project of Zimbabwe (MMPZ) has publicly lambasted two state-owned media outlets for failing to fairly report the story on war veterans. MMPZ said Zimbabwe Broadcasting Corporation's 2 March news bulletin did not air Home Affairs Secretary Dumiso Dabengwa's order for all war veterans to immediately leave squatted farms. The organisation also condemned state-owned Zimbabwe Newspapers Ltd for 'giving prominence only to the voice of the government, the war veterans and their leader'. The Commercial Farmers' Union (CFU) attacked the ZBC for partiality after the station refused to air on 17 March CFU advertisements of a High Court ruling forcing war veterans to leave the farms. The High Court ruling stated the CFU could advertise the decision four times a day for three successive days. The ZBC eventually complied on 24

March. (MISA)

On 29 March the Supreme Court ordered the police commissioner to investigate claims that the military tortured two journalists in January 1999. *Standard* editor **Mark Chavunduka** and chief reporter **Ray Choto** filed a civil case against the police force for failing to investigate their claims of torture (*Index* 3/1999, 4/1999, 6/1999, 1/2000, 2/2000). The Supreme Court reserved judgment on 20 March on a second application challenging the constitutional validity of charges brought against the pair under Section 50 of the Law and Maintenance Act for publishing false information likely to cause fear and alarm. The journalists argued in court on 20 March that Section 50 contravenes the constitution, which safeguards freedom of expression and the right to a fair trial. The trial continues. (MISA)

A *Daily News* crew was detained for two hours by ZANU-PF youths brandishing iron bars and golf clubs on 7 April. The youths threatened to kill features editor **Nyasha Nyakunu**, photographer **Tsvangirai Mukwazhi** and driver **Shadreck Muchecheni** for 'sympathising' with white commercial farmers. The youths confiscated the crew's equipment and press cards, before interrogating them in a farmhouse just outside Harare. The crew were set free shortly afterwards. (MISA) ❏

Compiled by: Melanie Clark, Shifa Rahman, Daniel Rogers (Africa); Ben Carrdus, Rupert Clayton, Heidi Joyce, Andrew Kendle (Asia); William Escofet, Daniel Rogers (south and central America); Arif Azad, Gill Newsham, Neil Sammonds (Middle East); Humfrey Hunter (north America and Pacific); Steve Donachie (Britain and western Europe); Katy Seppard (eastern Europe and the Balkans).

Window Rock, Arizona, 9 March 2000. Navajo Nation President Kelsey Begaye casts his vote using a laptop computer outside the tribal headquarters – Credit: Jeff Topping/Newsmakers/Camera Press

The net curtain

**The battle for the future of the
Internet is not a simple tussle
between freedom and regulation.
A Mexican stand-off is developing
between communication, commerce
and control – those who want their
say, those who want to make it pay,
and those who say 'No way!'**

JOHN NAUGHTON

The invisible hand

Those whom the gods wish to destroy they first make complacent.
For some years now, the uncensored, anarchic freedom of speech
available on the Internet has been rightly celebrated as one of the
wonders of the age. Among its benefits is the fact that it has become
increasingly difficult for governments and official bodies to restrict the
circulation of awkward information.

In the 1980s, for example, the British government successfully used
legal methods to prevent *Spycatcher* – the memoirs of a former MI5
officer named Peter Wright, who alleged that MI5 had conspired to
undermine the Wilson government in the 1960s – from being read by
British citizens, even though the book had been widely published
abroad. Newspapers that tried to publish excerpts were injuncted and
British residents who wished to read Wright's allegations had to resort to
absurd measures like making a day-trip to the Irish Republic to obtain a
copy.

This would be unimaginable today. At the first sign of a British or
European injunction, the contents of the book would appear on a webserver in the US where they would enjoy the protection of the First
Amendment and be available to anyone with a browser and an Internet
connection.

Governments have traditionally been ambivalent about the Internet.
On the one hand, they desire the economic benefits that it brings. On
the other, they are deeply apprehensive about its uncontrollability. To
date, however, they have found it difficult to do much about the latter –
and when they have tried they have generally come unstuck. A few
administrations – notably the US, Singapore and China – made early
attempts to interfere with net freedoms, but their efforts were
conceptually and technically inept.

For example, in 1996, the US enacted the Communications Decency
Act, a statute that sought to regulate Internet communications but

Beijing, 5 June 1999. A child walks past a huge computer display in a shopping mall – Credit: Peter Rogers/Newsmakers/Camera Press

quickly impaled itself on the First Amendment and was declared unconstitutional in just over a year. 'The Internet may fairly be regarded,' wrote one of the judges involved in the case, 'as a never-ending worldwide conversation. The government may not, through the CDA, interrupt that conversation. As the most participatory form of mass speech yet developed, the Internet deserves the highest protection from governmental intrusion.'

The Supreme Court's judgment on the CDA delighted the Internet community – loosely defined as the group of people who were using the network before the explosion of the World Wide Web in 1995 turned it into a mass medium – because it reinforced their libertarian philosophy that combines hostility to government with contempt for its ineptitude. The shambles of the CDA seemed to confirm the community's view that government had no business interfering in the online world.

The assumption implicit in this ideology – that government poses the main threat to liberty – is a badge of honour among cyber-libertarians everywhere. What has made this ideology so powerful – or at any rate so intimidating to governments – is that it is enthusiastically shared by a very different and increasingly powerful social grouping: the e-commerce lobby that seeks to turn the Internet into the greatest money-making machine in history.

It would be difficult to imagine two more dissimilar groups. Cyber-libertarians tend to be uninterested in – if not actively hostile to – commerce. Steeped in the 'high-tech gift culture' that is the Internet, they tend to be technically adept as well as utopian and idealistic, in the best sense of those terms. They believe that 'information wants to be free' and derive great comfort from John Gilmore's famous observation that 'the net sees censorship as damage and routes around it'. The e-commerce lobby, in contrast, certainly does not believe that information ought to be free; in fact, it would like to be able to charge us every time we view a website. And the main reason it wants to keep the government out of cyberspace is that government means taxation and regulation and generally interference with the God-given right of Stanford alumni to make as much money as they damn well please.

In the last two years, we have begun to realise that this unholy alliance of libertarianism and business may pose a bigger threat than government to the freedoms we cherish on the net. The man who has done most to alert us to the perils ahead is a Harvard law professor named Lawrence Lessig. He is by background a constitutional lawyer and he looks at the issues posed by the Internet much as, two centuries earlier, James Madison looked at the challenges of devising a new constitution for the United States. Madison is rightly regarded as 'the father of the constitution'. It was he, for example, who drew up the plan whereby the government was to be composed of three separate divisions – legislative, executive and judicial. He was also the main architect of the Bill of Rights and of the first ten amendments to the US Constitution, framed during the first session of the first Congress, of which he was a member.

Like Madison, Lessig is acutely aware of the fact that liberties can only be preserved by the deliberate balancing of opposing forces. In a remarkable, passionate, sobering book, *Code: and other laws of Cyberspace*, he argues that those who believe that the expansion of e-commerce and the movement of public discourse on to the net will increase our freedom (as consumers and citizens) are badly mistaken. Lessig believes that the cyber-libertarians and Silicon Valley lobbyists who (for their different reasons) maintain that government has no role on the net are creating a dangerous constitutional vacuum. 'When we see the path that cyberspace is on,' he writes, 'we see that much of the "liberty" present at cyberspace's founding will vanish in its future. Values that we now consider fundamental will not necessarily remain. Freedoms that were foundational will slowly disappear'.

Lessig's argument is predicated on a simple insight: the freedoms of cyberspace are determined by the technical architecture of the net. There is a famous *New Yorker* cartoon that captures this central principle in a single image. It shows two dogs in front of a computer. One animal is explaining to the other that what he loves about the net is that 'nobody knows you're a dog'. Although every computer connected to the Internet has to have a unique (and therefore traceable) address at the time of its connection, the architecture does not require that the *person* using that machine should be identifiable. Nor does the network specify or control what that person may use the net for. All the network does is to forward data packets from their source to their destination. The fact that those packets may be fragments of a pornographic or seditious Web page, a love letter, junk mail, a video sequence, part of a telephone conversation or an MP3 music file is entirely immaterial to the Internet.

The decentralised, permissive structure of the net is what gives it its resilience and what has enabled it to spread like a virus through society. In the case of the Internet, said Mitch Kapor, founder of the Electronic Frontier Foundation, 'architecture is politics'. The absence of centralised control that makes it less vulnerable to attack also means that anyone can join in: all you need is access to a computer which 'speaks' the technical language of the net. And the fact that access to the network does not depend on *who* you are provides the basis for the amazing freedom of expression that characterises cyberspace. The anonymity it allows is what enables people to speak in ways that they could not (or would not) in 'real' space.

What has all this to do with e-commerce? Well, the problem is that a space in which nobody knows you're a dog is not an environment in which one can safely trade. E-commerce requires security, authentication and confirmation of transactions. An online trader needs to know with whom he or she is dealing; messages and transactions have to be secure from surveillance and interference; ways have to be found for appending 'digital signatures', which have legal validity, to electronic documents; and so on.

Now of course there are technical solutions to all of these requirements, though many of them are currently rather clumsy to implement. But the economic imperatives of online commerce are so compelling that vast improvements in the necessary protocols are under way. An entire new technical architecture to facilitate e-commerce is being created, in other words, ready to be grafted on to the older, libertarian architecture of the net. And therein lies the danger.

The implication is that the Internet in 2005, say – let us call it Net2005 – could look very different from the Internet as it was in 1995. The old, libertarian layer will still exist, but a new layer – the e-commerce stratum – will sit above it. And the values implicit in the architecture of this new layer will be radically different from those implicit in the old one.

The key difference will be that the new layer will use the technical facilities of the old layer to eliminate anonymity and erode privacy. To understand how this will happen, you have to know something about how the net operates. At present, every machine on the network has a unique address for the duration of its connection, and every transaction that machine conducts leaves a record. When you request a Web page from a site for example, the address of the requesting machine and the nature of its request are logged by the server. Anyone who runs a website can, therefore, find out the address of every machine which has accessed his or her site. What they cannot ascertain, however, is the identity of the *persons* who initiated those accesses.

But the new e-commerce layer could change all that. It would enable sites, for example, to refuse access to people who refused – or were unable – to provide a digital signature authenticating their identity. Once admitted, everything those authenticated visitors did – which Web pages they viewed, and for how long, which items they purchased, what they appeared to be most interested in and so on – can be logged against their real identities. And, of course, the information thus gathered could be sold or disclosed to other agencies, all without the subjects' knowledge or consent. And because all the information gathered within such a layer would be in machine-readable form, it would be technologically and economically feasible to compile massive databases on the online behaviour of named individuals.

The erosion of privacy implicit in such systems is an obvious danger. Less obvious, perhaps, is their potential for limiting access and widening the 'digital divide' between those who have a foothold in the new economy and those who do not. Apologists for the new e-commerce layer point out that nobody will be forced to have a digitally-authenticated signature and that they don't have to visit any site which requires one. True. But then there is no obligation on anyone to have a credit card either – but try renting a car or checking into an hotel nowadays without one.

Add to the authentication threat the provisions for digital copyright which the e-commerce lobby has in store for us and you have the makings of an Orwellian nightmare. When the Web first took off and it became easy to copy any text and distribute it globally, publishers (and in some cases authors) feared that it spelled ruination for them. It was, they argued, a charter for intellectual piracy – the equivalent of putting a photocopier and a printing press into every home. It hasn't turned out like that, but you can see why they were alarmed because, with Net1995, everything they feared was technically possible.

But spool forward a few years and change the architecture to that of Net2005 and an entirely new scenario presents itself. Every document published on the Web can be encrypted, so that only readers who have paid for a decryption key can access it. Alternatively, an unencrypted document can have a secret 'digital watermark' embedded in it, enabling publishers to tell at once whether a given digital copy is a legitimate, paid-for, version or a pirated one. And even if the document is published free, unencrypted and unmarked, on a net where authentication protocols are in place the publisher can determine the precise identity of every single person who accesses the document online – and sell that information to other customers. Within such an architecture, the practice of anonymous reading – one of the great bulwarks of intellectual freedom – could be rendered impossible, at least in relation to online documents.

The biggest threat posed by the coming hegemony of e-commerce, however, is that the entire thing is being driven by the needs of business rather than the interests of citizens or society. Many governments appear to have accepted the view that their presence in cyberspace should be as minimal as possible, and most have confined their efforts to clearing a path through the legislative undergrowth (for example, by passing laws that make digital signatures legal) or gibbering – as in the case of the current British government – about making their jurisdictions 'friendly to e-commerce', whatever that might mean.

The result is that a new Internet is evolving solely under commercial pressure. It will be a virtual space in which many of us will increasingly spend part of our work and leisure lives, and in which much of the daily business of our economies will be transacted. But it will also be a place where there is no privacy, little consumer or employee protection and – because of the abdication of governments – virtually no regulation. There will be no concern for civil rights, and no attempt to balance the needs of society against the commercial imperatives of large and powerful corporations.

The inescapable implication is that cyberspace – the most gloriously open, uncensored and unregulated public space in human history – could easily become the most controlled environment imaginable. That is the fear that pervades Lessig's magnificent, sombre book: 'The invisible hand of cyberspace is building an architecture that is quite the opposite of what it was at cyberspace's birth. The invisible hand, through commerce, is constructing an architecture that perfects control.' George Orwell feared that we would be destroyed by the things we fear. Aldous Huxley thought we would be destroyed by the things we love. The logic of Lessig's argument is that both were right. ❑

John Naughton, *naughton@pobox.com, leads the Open University's 'Going Digital' project. He is a fellow of Wolfson College Cambridge, the* Observer's *Internet columnist and the author of* A Brief History of the Future: the Origins of the Internet *(Weidenfeld & Nicolson, 1999)*

JOHN GITTINGS

Fever pitch

Will the Internet bring democracy to the Chinese people as Bill Clinton has eagerly argued; or will Beijing manage to keep tight controls on it; or will it make any difference either way?

The 'Web fever' China is now experiencing has similar characteristics to previous 'fevers' – Mao, development, religion, etc – which have swept through the student population and new urban middle class in recent years. The difference is that this time it is shared by many outside commentators who see China's exponential growth in Web access as the most important development since the 1989 student democracy movement.

Bill Clinton has regarded himself as an authority on the growth of the Internet in China, ever since he hailed it during his visit there in 1998 as the precursor of political change. At that time there were less than two million Web users in the whole country; now there are nearly ten million. Democracy has gone backwards in the same time but Clinton remains seduced by his own argument – or at least regards it as an effective way of winning over congressional opponents to China's entry into the World Trade Organisation. 'When you get all this telecommunications revolution permanently manifest in China,' he declared on 29 March, 'they will not be able to control the Internet, they will not be able to control access to information, they will not be able to control freedom of information. It (China) will become a more free country and a more open country ...'

By a bizarre coincidence, the Internet was invoked by the official Chinese news agency – within a day of the President's interview – to prove the opposite point. Freedom of information, Xinhua insisted, is fully protected in China, citing 'the rapid growth in the Internet' as its first example. By the end of 1999, China already had nearly nine million users and 15,000 websites. How wrong the US was to claim that Chinese human rights have deteriorated in the past year: they were getting better all the time!

There has indeed been an Internet explosion, the latest phase in a computer revolution which itself is only five or six years old. Zhongguancun, in the north of Beijing, known everywhere as China's Silicon Valley, has engulfed a village of brick and mud houses where street sellers still cry out their wares. Until the 1980s most of the surrounding land was farmed by peasants. Now Zhongguancun has launched Phase Two of an expansion plan. Where students from nearby Beijing University used to cycle along narrow paths between the fields, billboards advertise high-tech companies and new Internet sites.

True, the Internet does open fresh windows to free information and argument as fast as Beijing tries to nail them shut. And ordinary Chinese are able to access the Web without too much difficulty: official efforts to build firewalls against the import of undesirable news are half-hearted and ineffectual. Yet none of this means that China is about to surf its way into a new political culture.

The numbers recorded in a survey by the government-sponsored China Internet Network Information Centre are indeed impressive and are judged by an independent specialist writing for ChinaOnline.com (the best source for Chinese Internet development) to be reasonably accurate. They show that 3.5 million computers could access the Internet by the end of 1999, with a ratio of 2.5 people to each computer totalling around 8.9 million users. The fourfold increase in less than two years will be dwarfed if projections for the future are anything like accurate. These suggest that by the middle of this decade China will have several tens of millions of Internet users, outstripping Japan and possibly the US as well.

It is also true – and has already been shown in the past – that IT can assist the flow of independent news and views. In 1989, during the student democracy movement, overseas supporters used faxes to transmit to China foreign news reports (unfortunately, not always accurate) of what was happening on the streets of Beijing.

The spread of international direct dialling in the 1990s has meant that overseas human rights organisations can obtain immediate information on strikes, demonstrations and other protests even in the most remote parts of the country. (Again unfortunately, this does not mean that the

news which is then retransmitted by the groups abroad is always reliable.) Indeed such telephone calls, which can be made from commercial roadside phones, are harder for the authorities to trace than emails.

The expanded use of the Internet will clearly also help activists at home and abroad exchange information and ideas, but does this justify the Clinton vision? The great proportion of China's dial-up subscribers, says ChinaOnline, 'are actually small and medium-sized business users'. Customers in Internet cafés – which can, in any case, be more easily monitored – are more likely to be interested in game-playing than politics. Internet access is also very uneven across China. Six cities or provinces shared 60% of China's total users last year, with Beijing, Shanghai and Guangdong province alone accounting for 45%. Most users were male, single, aged 30 and below and university educated. Not surprisingly, the number of peasants or ordinary workers with Web access as shown by the survey was too small to be statistically reliable.

How far the Internet might become a vehicle for free information depends both on the degree of censorship and on user preference. The main government-approved sites are careful not to disseminate foreign reports or comment on their Chinese-language pages – though some will carry western agency material in English. 'News is a really sensitive area,' says a senior website executive. 'We ask ourselves all the time how we can develop without being shut down. It's like playing a game with no rules. They just come back later and say "You can't do it".'

Determined users can access overseas Chinese-language sites carrying sensitive material without too much difficulty, but how many will wish to do so? Most of the sites concentrate on personal and lifestyle themes, seeking to respond to the dominant interests of many young urban Chinese with money to spend and little interest in political affairs. These are after all commercial sites which are struggling to make money in a very competitive market. All of them have now latched on to the latest electronic vogue, announcing their intention to embark upon e-commerce, even though the Chinese banking system is nowhere near being able to provide the financial support needed for online payment.

One typical site is the high-profile *Zhaodaola* – the name means 'I've found it!'. *Zhaodaola* is backed by a US company owned by right-wing evangelist Pat Robertson, but it preaches a very different religion, describing itself as a 'lifestyle portal'. 'A person has to spend much time looking for something,' says the general manager Yu Hongyan, 'whether it be a job, a friend, a house or a lover. People in China are aiming for a better life. We are entitled to the quality you get in the US and Japan. We're targeting the 20 to 35-year-olds and trying to attract more women. That's why we have a special channel called Real Women – as well as another one called Macho Men.'

After trying unsuccessfully to fight it, official Chinese policy has now moved towards joining the Web. In January, new rules published by the State Secrecy Bureau imposed tough security checks, and new regulations required foreign firms to register their encryption software. But the secrecy checks are already being ignored, and the encryption requirement has been relaxed to conform to WTO regulations.

The government also dithered for months over whether to let Chinese Internet companies list their shares overseas with open disagreement between different sections of the bureaucracy. Listing has finally been allowed, subject to a face-saving device by which the site's China-based assets are split off from the parent company. Even this device may not survive WTO entry.

Sina.com, the leading Chinese portal and the first to list, has set up a foreign-based firm as its listing vehicle which technically will not have ownership relations with the mainland provider. But it will be linked via another company which operates the mainland site.

The exponential growth of the Web in China has impressed the Chinese leadership as much as Clinton. 'The Party has stayed in power because it is a "vanguard force",' President Jiang Zemin told the National People's Congress last month. 'To continue to be so, senior cadres must equip themselves better by learning Internet technology.'

While Clinton sees the Internet as a Trojan Horse for western ideas, the Chinese leadership is intent on harnessing it to launch a new revolution in technology. The results in both areas are likely to be more modest than either president claims. And for hundreds of millions of Chinese away from the main urban centres, this new form of ideological struggle means very little compared with their continuing struggle for the essentials of life. ❏

John Gittings *is East Asia correspondent for the* Guardian *and* Observer. *His latest book is* China Through the Sliding Door *(Simon & Schuster 1999)*

● *It is reported that* Index*'s website is now blocked from China* ❏

ERIK SCHECTER

Surfing the secular

Forced to choose between a rabbinical ban and feeding their families, ultra-Orthodox Jews are voting with their mice

'Look at this!' exclaims Haim, recoiling. 'I try to find a technology site, and this is what I get.' A banner on his screen shows three naked women caressing themselves. Shmuel, Haim's colleague, shifts uncomfortably and chooses not to peer over.

Shmuel and Haim are programmers at Versaware, a high-tech firm in Jerusalem's Talpiot Industrial Zone that publishes electronic books on the Internet. Merely by doing his job, Shmuel is defying his rabbi. On 8 January, the rabbinical court of Edah Haredit, an umbrella group representing the most fanatic five per cent of the ultra-Orthodox population, denounced the Internet as 'a deadly poison' which 'burns souls' and outlawed its use.

Haim does not follow an Edah rabbi and is in greyer territory. While mainstream ultra-Orthodox clergy are unhappy about the Internet, they have stopped short of banning it. Instead, in a recent ruling, Rabbis Yosef Shalom Eliashiv and Aaron Yehuda Leib Sheinman forbade the Internet at home and urged their flocks to minimise its use at work. 'Professionals who need the Internet for their livelihood,' they declared, 'must find every means possible to limit its use.' Although Rabbi Ovadiah Yosef, spiritual mentor of the ultra-Orthodox Shas party, did not sign the ruling, his aides say that he backs it. Shas does not maintain a website and has no plans to launch one.

Ironically, the ruling was posted on the Web by one ultra-Orthodox news service, though its principal means of publication, in accordance with custom, is in large type on posters pasted on the walls in ultra-Orthodox neighbourhoods like Jerusalem's Geulah and Me'ah She'arim.

For decades, ultra-Orthodox rabbis have maintained a largely successful ban on TV to shield their communities from far milder erotica

and violent imagery than is available over the Internet. So the new bans
come as no surprise. The trouble is that high-tech work – which
inevitably involves the Internet – is becoming ever more integral to the
ultra-Orthodox economy. Increasing numbers of male and, especially,
female members have flooded into information technology, because the
lack of a university education is no barrier and, in some cases, they can
work from home. At present, there are 20–35,000 computers in Israel's
80-100,000 ultra-Orthodox households, according to Shai Horovitz,
spokesman for the Manof Jewish Information Service, an ultra-
Orthodox media relations firm.

For those who follow the letter of the Edah's ruling, there is no
alternative: they must give up their jobs. But a significant number of
people for the first time must now choose between pleasing their rabbis
and feeding their families – and it's the rabbis who are coming off
second-best.

The Web's route to virtual sex and images of violence is not all that
troubles the rabbis. They fear the Web because it delivers the secular
world in its entirety into ultra-Orthodox living rooms. 'Some sections of
Me'ah She'arim have managed to shut themselves off from the modern
world,' says Ezra Rosenfeld, US-born director of the Tzomet Institute, a
non-profit organisation that finds technological solutions to problems of
Jewish law. 'TVs are banned; secular newspapers aren't read; people don't
read secular books, they don't go to the movies. Now the rabbis are
trying to block the net.'

'The rabbis have taken a heroic decision and I hope the ban succeeds,'
says Rabbi Shmuel Jacobovits, director of Ura Kevodi, the Jerusalem-
based Haredi Association for the Study of Contemporary Issues.
'Globalisation tends, if not to eradicate moral strength, then to weaken
it.' As a forum for so many different points of view, so many lifestyle
choices, asserts Jacobovits, the son of the late Chief Rabbi of Britain,
'the Internet represents permissiveness, superficiality and the free play of
ideas at the expense of any particular idea of standing firm.'

Other ultra-Orthodox figures, while endorsing the rabbis' concerns,
fear that calls to boycott the Web have come too late and that, while
there will not be open defiance, the ruling will be seen as an ideal, rather
than a realistic proposal. 'The view from the street is that the rabbis
missed the opportunity,' says Yehudah Meshi-Zahav, who handles Edah
relations with the outside world. 'Computer use is ten per cent higher

among ultra-Orthodox than the general public. Most houses already have a computer.' The best hope, he says, is that the ruling may dampen rampant enthusiasm for the Internet. 'Maybe in the margins, in certain groups, it will be less talked about.'

Indeed, elaborates Bar-Ilan University sociologist Menachem Friedman, the very fact that the non-Edah ultra-Orthodox stopped short of an all-out ban, and 'adopted a compromise position ... underlines the recognition that a complete ban is unrealistic and counter-productive economically.' The initial impact of the rabbis' call appears to bear this out. Netvision, one of Israel's leading Internet providers, has seen no closing of accounts in ultra-Orthodox areas like B'nai Brak and Liat Ya'ari at Aquanet, a smaller provider, tells the same story: 'We haven't had a single customer asking to be disconnected because of the rulings.'

Posters announcing the rabbinical rulings are prominently displayed near the Me'ah She'arim branch of Torah Scholar Software, where net-related software is for sale. And at the Netcafe in the boisterous Russian Compound, about three blocks from the edge of Me'ah She'arim, there are plenty of ultra-Orthodox youngsters mixing with the modern-Orthodox around the terminals. Gavriel and Avraham, two former Chicagoans who study at the Mir Yeshivah, are checking out the latest Bulls scores. 'We shouldn't be doing this,' says Gavriel, 'but we're diehard fans. The rabbis are right to a certain extent. We should be learning. Once you get on the net, the *yetzer hara* (the evil instinct) can take over.'

Back at Versaware, Shmuel reads over an Edah handbill calling for a total abstention – something that would end his career if he obeyed. 'We haven't yet gotten to their standard,' he says sadly. 'If I were at that spiritual level, I would pack up and learn [Torah] all day. But, and I'm not sure if this is right,' he goes on, 'there are 70 faces to the Torah. The tribe of Zebulun supported the tribe of Issachar while it sat and learned Torah.' In fact, members of this latterday 'tribe of Issachar' are embracing the net, using websites to spread their message. The Chabad movement, for instance, maintains dozens, if not hundreds of sites, in English, Hebrew and other languages. Visitors to *www.chabad.org* are welcomed to 'Chabad-Lubavitch in Cyberspace' with a picture of the late Rabbi Menachem Mendel Schneerson and a hassidic 'Thought for the Day'.

Ultimately, Bar-Ilan's Friedman believes that, rabbinical orders notwithstanding, the Internet will infiltrate secular ideas into the ultra-Orthodox community, and this will chip away at people. That, he says, is the price the community must pay for enjoying the modern conveniences of the West. 'You can't say "I'll enjoy the western world up to a certain limit",' he argues. 'In five, ten years, the Internet will be used to fulfil basic needs like paying your bills. It'll be impossible to control access to it.'

In fact, when asked to fax a text of the rabbinical rationale for the Internet rulings, spokesman Shai Horovitz of the Manof information centre replied: 'Sorry, I don't have that in front of me. Could you check our website at *www.manof.org.il*. It's there.' ❏

Erik Schechter is a staff writer for the Jerusalem Report

BRAD GLOSSERMAN

Reversal of fortune

With a little help from friends abroad, Japanese campaigners are beginning to change diehard attitudes at home – and the law is following suit

Can a single statistic move a parliament? It certainly seemed that way last year when the Japanese diet, after years of inaction that bordered on defiance of international norms, passed legislation to combat child pornography. It is one of the toughest packages of laws in the world. Supporters at home and abroad marvelled at the change of heart even as they struggled, unsuccessfully, to explain it.

The Japanese bill makes it illegal for anyone in Japan, or any Japanese travelling overseas, to pay for sexual intercourse with children under the age of 18 – commonly described as 'sex tourism'. It also bans the production, distribution and sale of pornographic material featuring children. Japanese comics, *manga*, are excluded from the scope of the latter provisions. (Sales of *manga* topped ¥500billion last year – $4.5billion – and the industry has huge clout with parliament.) Perry Aftab, executive director of Cyber Angels and one of the leaders in the fight against child pornography, calls the law 'very strict', high praise from a sceptic. 'A year ago, I would have laughed at the prospect of Japan passing this law. There was no way. But this has happened faster than anyone dreamed would happen.'

Why the change? Combatants in the fight against kiddie porn credit the embarrassment that resulted when Interpol said that 80% of the child pornography found on the Internet originated in Japan. The figure was quickly picked up by the media and routinely trotted out whenever the subject was discussed. Japan, ever sensitive to such criticism, moved quickly to pass legislation that would repair the damage to the country's international image.

It's a plausible theory, and one grounded in history. Traditionally, domestic reformers in Japan have relied on foreign pressure to bring about change in a society disposed to preserve the status quo. The phenomenon, *gaiatsu*, has been studied in depth in the context of international trade negotiations. According to this logic, the humiliation created by the Interpol statistic gave Japanese supporters of the new legislation the leverage they needed to break the political logjam.

It's elegant, but it isn't convincing. Japan was censured back in 1996, when an international conference in Stockholm labelled the country 'a distribution centre' for pornography involving minors. Moreover, the 80% figure, while eye-opening, isn't accurate. Aftab said maybe 40% of the kiddie porn on the Internet came from sites with Japanese addresses, but even then much of the material featured western children, which meant that it did not originate in Japan. The British group, Internet Watch Foundation, reports that Japan was the source of 19% of confirmed child pornography distributed over the Internet between 1996 and 1997.

That is not to say that child pornography isn't a problem in Japan. There have been international complaints about the ease with which such material can be found in Japan. The growth of the Internet has simply made Japan's willingness to tolerate the publication of this material more visible: the number of complaints from foreign law enforcement agencies has been growing in step with the penetration ratio of the Internet.

Still, it is a mistake to say that the push for reform came entirely from outside the country. The vocal and growing lobby for change had its hand strengthened by international pressures but was already making its voice heard. The key movers on the side of change are female politicians and activists horrified by the abuse that is behind the cartoon depictions of pornography. Japan has a huge comics industry whose products appeal to adults of all ages; the line between adult and pornography is easily blurred. 'These women saw the real children behind the cartoons and decided enough was enough,' said Aftab. 'They decided to educate legislators.'

Their efforts were aided by a larger shift within the country. Japan is in the midst of a historic transition, grappling with its place in the world and within Asia. But Japan's relations with the region are tainted by

Japan's role there in WWII and its willingness – or not – to take responsibility for its acts during the war, chief among them, the legacy of the 'comfort women', mainly Koreans, forced into prostitution (*Index* 3/95).

As Japan tries to chart a new foreign policy course, it is being forced to confront its ugly deeds – and their modern-day variant, the sex tours in South-East Asia, in which underage children are often the prey. Some Japanese credit stories of Japanese men being prosecuted overseas for sex with minors with forcing the nation to confront the issue. The Japanese representatives of End Child Prostitution in Asia, a Bangkok-based NGO, have been key movers in the campaign against child porn in the country. Akihiro Hagio, Japan's representative to UNICEF, explained that 'Japanese tourists have a very bad name ... anyone who goes to South-East Asia can see that'.'

At the same time, Japan is undergoing a demographic transition. Women, traditionally treated as second-class citizens, are becoming more assertive and less accepting of their place in society. One dimension of this new outlook is the increasing attention given to *seku hara* or sexual harassment. In a recent landmark case, a female campaign worker sued the governor of Osaka for molesting her in a vehicle during a rally. Despite his denials, she persisted in her charges and forced his resignation. The country's shrinking birth rate – the result of a reluctance on the part of women to get married and shoulder all the burdens that entails – has forced the government to shift its attitude.

Although it is, strictly speaking, a different issue, the fight against pornography is another part of this new outlook. The movement was given real impetus a few years ago when *enjo kosai*, compensated dating, received a lot of attention in the media. Reports that high-school girls were engaging in what was basically prostitution to finance their hunger for brand-name goods – Prada handbags, Hermès scarves – outraged many and prompted a high-profile media campaign against the practice. As virtually all the participants were under the age of 18, the focus slid towards the exploitation of children more generally.

The key players were again women, this time politicians, unwilling to tolerate the male-oriented standards. They are widely credited with keeping the issue alive in the traditionally male-dominated parliament. Sumiko Shimuzu, a Social Democratic Party member of the lower house, explained the linkage: 'The popularity of telephone clubs, where

'Hentai' image – Credit: origin unknown

schoolgirls contact customers for sex, and the high incidence of schoolgirl prostitution in Japan are a big social problem ... that goes hand in hand with the sexual exploitation of children.'

Part of the problem stems from Japan's image of the ideal woman, which tends to be younger than in most other parts of the world; part can be ascribed to a cultural framework fundamentally different from that of the West, say Japanese commentators. However, the speed with which Japan's law enforcement bodies are pursuing their new task appears to give the lie to the latter theory. Indeed, says Aftab, 'Japan has one of the top five cyber-crime law enforcement agencies in the world. They are going so fast it is extraordinary. They are really committed to making a difference.' ❏

Brad Glosserman *is a Japan-based journalist who frequently writes on Internet issues*

ANDREW WASLEY

Fr Sava's stained window

During his recent tour of Britain, the press came out in force to hear a Serbian Orthodox priest from Kosovo, a man called the 'cybermonk' by media analysts, such was the power of his Internet presence during last year's Kosovo war

Throughout the 78 nights of NATO bombing, Father Sava Janjic and his team of trainee monks bombarded western journalists with email updates from their 12th-century monastery in Decani, western Kosovo, providing what was regarded as one of the few sources of impartial information.

Fr Sava used his podium to stress the importance of the Internet as a medium for dialogue and a tool for 'building the foundations of a stable, multicultural Kosovo'. But reporters were frustrated the priest did not address pithier questions. 'Here we had the man behind the screen who supplied [the western media] with so much, and he appeared reluctant to divulge any information about himself or his background,' commented one.

Born in 1965 in Dubrovnik, Fr Sava grew up in Trebinje, Bosnia-Herzogovina and later studied English before entering the Orthodox Church. He started to work on computers while secretary to the Bishop of Raska-Prizren. In the Balkans, he is largely credited as the priest who put the Church on the Web: his Decani website has existed since 1997 though it was only in the build-up to NATO's bombing that the site attracted the attention of information-hungry journalists and others.

While the Internet output of both the KLA and Serbian information ministry was dismissed as nationalist propaganda, Fr Sava's effort was greeted by the BBC as 'a breath of fresh air among murky water'. The *Guardian* called it 'news not spin'. Detailed accounts of the atrocities committed by all sides were broadcast daily over the Decani site, and via email. Then came the stories about the monk who sheltered terrified civilians and rose at 1am to pray and go online. As one enthusiastic US commentator put it: 'The media have found their modern-day Schindler.'

A year on, the Decani monks are much quieter. The site is still there but the emphasis has shifted. Now the opening pages take the browser to the desecration of Orthodox religious sites and artefacts; Kosovo Albanians are branded 'thugs' and 'plunderers'; accounts of atrocities are confined to those attributed to the KLA and its 'outlaws'. There is little or no mention of the barbarities carried out by the Serbian police or army.

Some suggest that the change in slant is a result of the Decani monks adapting their Internet presence to match the changed political situation. 'NATO's ground intervention last summer brought with it thousands of news crews, opening up a region that had previously been the almost exclusive preserve of Decani,' said Desan Brasic, a Serbian freelance journalist in Sarajevo. 'Newspapers and television channels had little need of the Decani news providers once they could see with their own eyes. More important perhaps,' he continues, 'the Kosovo Serbs, for whom the Decani site was originally constructed, are now more dispersed [than when bombing began]. The new emphasis on national identity and Serbian suffering is possibly an attempt to provide a rallying point for such people.'

Though updated direct from the Decani monastery, the site also advertises addresses in the US and abroad, the result of several high-profile trips by Fr Sava since the end of the war. 'It is quite possible that powerful figures in the Serb community at large are manipulating Decani through the back door to suit their own purposes' says Irene De Monte, a US political commentator. 'Websites are far easier to manipulate – politically speaking – than other forms of media, such as newspapers, which often have strict editorial conditions attached, not that these presented much obstacle to the Milosevic government. ❏

Andrew Wasley is a journalist specialising in media and human rights issues. Fr Sava's site is located at www.decani.yunet.com

Cytopias

Would-be citizens of nations without a land to call their own are staking out their territory in cyberspace

Our website has proved to be an economical and effective tool. Everyone can access it in any part of the world if they have a computer. They can act on it and pass it on. It saves a lot of money because one person can do what was previously done by many offices all over the world. There's also uniformity in the presentation. I like to keep the site simple, with not too many graphics, so that it's easy to download, easy to view and is user-friendly.
www.tibet.com

The Web provides an opportunity to tell our story to a larger audience which in many cases simply doesn't know that Sweden has a native people [the Sami]. It also informs our various groups of tribes. To some degree it seems to be successful, though not as much as originally thought. The interest was higher originally in 1996 when the website was created – so it seems that my presentation is beginning to get lost in the commercial 'noise' of the contemporary Internet.
www.boreale.se, www.samefolket.se

Our website provides a wide range of contacts for people who may be interested in the Taino Native American Indian heritage of the Caribbean and Florida Diaspora. An open Internet forum helps promote awareness and interest for our Jatibonicu Taino tribal nation's educational and cultural non-profit organisations. The site serves as a secondary resource along with faxes and snail mail.
www.hartford-hwp.com/taino

We are building a new country in the Caribbean. All promotion has been done with our website and email. As a result, we have received a great deal of publicity and news coverage. We have over 700 citizens now and will begin construction in July. This could not have

been done before the Internet. My government is scattered all over the world, and we communicate by email and telephone.
www.new-utopia.com

We are using the Web to highlight our Kashmir Cause and tell the communities in the world what is going on and about the function of the UN regarding Kashmir. We are gaining a lot of benefits; we are able to tell the real facts, and what is going wrong. The Web is a better means of communication, it is free of cost, it makes the world 'A Global Village'. It's up to a person how much he benefits from it. We could not convey our message in the world without spending millions of dollars. Our Web is doing this at a nominal cost.
www.klc.org.pk

The crisis in Chiapas will not be solved in cyberspace, yet the Internet can be a powerful tool for activism and information dissemination (hence, the page's existence).
www.ezln.org

The Kingdom of Talossa is a real nation in the real world, and is far older than the Internet ... a physical country – one which all people, on and off the Internet, are invited to join! Because of Talossa's relative antiquity and status, many online 'micronations' view Talossa with jealousy and animosity. It's something we're quite proud of. Freedom of the press is very important in Talossa. Most Talossan newspapers and newsletters are online.
www.talossa.com

If we rely on mass media to learn of Kurdistan, we find only a few scant, bleak images: tanks rolling down a dusty road, a fleeing populace clinging to a mountain, skirmishing troops perched on a scrubby hill. Little information makes for narrow vision. Happily, as more and more Kurdish sites appear on the Internet, better images are being shared.
www.krg.org ❏

Compiled by Natasha Schmidt

ROHAN JAYASEKERA

Waiting for the kingdom

Nations in cyberspace are no substitute for the real thing

W ould-be citizens of nations without a land to call their own are staking out their territory in cyberspace. Leaderships in exile, like the Sri Lankan Tamils or the Kurds of Turkey, sit in cyberspace as De Gaulle and Sikorski sat in London during WWII, waiting for their dominions. Meantime, landless Palestinians from the West Bank of the Jordan and Padanians from the north bank of the Po are using the Web to kit themselves out with the trappings of nationhood.

Some of this virtual nation building is as flimsy and irrelevant as you'd expect from a virtual government; some smacks of delusion. Italy's Northern League site clicks off with a front and back picture of a future Padanian passport. Several US websites are currently haggling over a constitution for a free republic on the planet Mars.

But for the Palestinians, at least, the effort has been constructive. The Internet has opened up a space for the development of a democratic civil society largely free of the bureaucracy and corruption that is strangling the putative Palestinian state in the real world. Palestine's feisty but marginalised parliament is making more of its role through its international links with other parliaments: foreign contacts made via the Web bring training, expertise and donor funds. Bir Zeit University's Open Borders Project is linking Palestinian-run West Bank towns with Palestinian-run Gaza, a feat that has so far eluded their real-time political leaders.

The Palestinian Authority puts plenty of pressure on its newspapers and broadcasters, but has, thus far, left the webcasters in peace. Its Internet interests have been largely confined to securing a country domain code along with a telephone country code and a national airline,

the more obvious trappings of nationhood. It finally caught up with the rest of the world and got its country domain last October; appropriately for an afterthought, it is to be '.ps'.

Useless it is too, both as national symbol and political tool. Israel's control of the nodes through which Palestinian Internet Service Providers (ISPs) reach the wider Web makes even more nonsense of the concept of a 'Palestinian' quarter of cyberspace. And should the Palestinian Authority ever think of trying to stop its dissidents holding forth on the Web, it will be all but powerless to prevent them dialling out via Egyptian, Jordanian and even Israeli phone numbers. That will leave the Palestinian Authority's buggers struggling to distinguish between fax calls and modem signals.

The Israeli security services solved that problem during the *intifada* by banning both fax and modem traffic. Simple enough; but not as simple as the way a Palestinian security chief resolved his opposition to a human rights journalism course I ran in Gaza in 1996: he sent in 12 men with AK47s to confiscate the computers. Even the dumbest secret policeman can silence the voice of minority nationalism and secession on the net by looking for the suspect with the large white box and screen on his desk. They are hard to hide. You can bury a cache of rifles for the resistance in Occupied Territory, but you'd be wise not to bury your Apple Powerbook with it.

Rebel forces temporarily bested by government special forces – the Kurdish PKK, for example – no longer head for the mountains, but drive to London and Geneva to plug in their laptops and regroup in cyberspace. But their opponents are following them. The Turkish secret services have set up a special team to track down PKK websites and email.

In April, pro-Serb hackers broke into domain name registrar Network Solutions to target websites serving Serbian pro-democracy groups, the breakaway former Yugoslav states and Serbia's truculent partner republic, Montenegro. One of the targeted sites, Montenegro.com, is physically run from Los Angeles, but is no more safe virtually than a site operated from Belgrade or Podgorica. Its owner claims he can trace the hackers back to Belgrade. The aim remains to stop separatists and national minorities from setting up virtual states in cyberspace as a prelude to the real thing in the real world. China moved smartly to sign up Taiwan.com before the Taiwanese government could do so, echoing in domain registration its policy towards Taiwan the island. 'This disputed ownership of cyberspace must be understood as a question of colonial motivations,' wrote *Wired* magazine's Michael Leventhal. 'The goal is to raise your flag on new territory in cyberspace, put your name (or the name you choose) on the "land". But whose land is it? Is the first person there the one with the right to claim it?'

On the Internet, people's nationalities are most commonly identified by their email addresses and the giveaway country code that Palestine put so much store by. The United States is the exception: its net citizens declining to make use of the '.us' suffix, settling for the non-national '.com', '.net' etc. Nowadays, a great proportion of names in the .com domain list are non-US; many companies outside the US make a virtue of their nationality by operating domains with national tags, whether for global business purposes, or to assert their non-US identity. The French, in particular, stress the use of their '.fr' identifier.

This national identity can be imported if necessary. The webpage provider GeoCities lists members' private homepages by 'neighbourhood' intended to indicate something of the members' character depending on whether his or her private webpage is situated in 'Soho', 'Paris' or some other place

All in all, the effect is schizophrenic; Web users celebrate the Internet's ability to transcend national borders, but fall over themselves to place themselves in corners of cyberspace with national identities. The reaction to the predominance of English on the Internet is equally divided. A 1999 survey of several million Web pages by the ExciteHome portal estimated that more than three-quarters were written in English. While English was initially celebrated as a lingua franca for the Web, its overarching use is today tagged as post-imperialist rather than post-modern.

By some estimates, of the 7,000 or so languages spoken around the world, only ten per cent will still be there by the end of the century. 'A language,' goes the saying, 'is only a dialect with an army.' Of an estimated 300 languages spoken in the Americas when Columbus landed, only 175 are still spoken; of those, only 20 are being transmitted to the next generation. The anglophone Web may be speeding up that process.

So here is another area for the Internet nationalist to work out his ambitions for his or her people. Linguistic nationalism has an honourable

Arnhem Land, Australia. Aboriginal women using an Apple laptop –
Credit: Penny Tweedie/Panos

record as a force for change in Czech and Hungarian lands in the 17th
and 18th centuries; a dishonourable record in Sri Lanka and South
Africa in the 1950s. Yet there are those on the Web who believe they
can save or make nations by first saving their linguistic culture.
Commenting on the former, Marek Kohn picks out the Pages Jerraiases
on the Internet, set up to serve the estimated 5,700 people who speak
the almost lost native dialect of the island of Jersey. Elsewhere, one Uldis
Balodis, he notes, has built a site devoted to the lost language and culture
of Livonia, which once thrived where Latvia now is. 'On the Livonian

links page there are nine links,' he writes, 'just one fewer than the number of native Livonian speakers in the real world.'

And when it comes to language, technological change can change things overnight. The development of Web browsers that display *kanji* characters narrowly saved the Japanese from the indignity of seeing their language 'latinised' for the Web, and just in time. Arabic, Cyrillic and a host of non-Latin languages running left to right and right to left are being helped by designers who fill the gaps which innovations like Unicode – the computer coding system for the world's alphabets, now standing at 50,000 characters and shortly to gain the 41 letters in the Etruscan alphabet – cannot cover.

Ironically, the greatest problem facing the virtual nation-builders is that their long-term contribution to nation-building remains just that: virtual. Their relevance applies only to those who combine commitment to their interpretation of national identity with ownership of a US$1,500 computer. Offline they may wither and die, as their naive enthusiasms are blunted by reality. Before the NATO strikes, the Kosovars built a parallel system of government and civil administration to serve the ethnic Albanians who boycotted the Serbian-run services. As a system, it might have been tailor-made for the Internet, but it was swiftly buried alive under the dead weight of the armed acronyms – UNMIK, OSCE, NATO, KFOR and UCK. For the Internet provides very limited security against the depredations of the real world. Web-savvy Turkish secret agents can pursue the PKK into the darker corners of cyberspace; Serbs pull the plug on Montenegrin webservers.

And for those who escape this kind of assault, the resultant isolation from the non-virtual world has its own price. It may leave the virtual leaders of virtual states, not as the new millennium's Charles de Gaulle, but as its Wladyslaw Sikorski, whose WWII Polish government in exile sat fruitlessly on in London, ignored for decades after his death. Ultimately the founders of virtual nations, like most Web users, really ought to get out more. ❏

Rohan Jayasekera
Index on Censorship *plans a programme of projects in 2000-2001 examining linguistic and cultural identity on the Web and its link to free expression*

SALIL TRIPATHI

Top dogging it

The Internet revolution is changing India's relationship to the business world: its IT companies are home-grown and earning big bucks – and its real money

There was a time when Shuvam Misra could enjoy the ride on a hovercraft across the harbour, from his home in Vashi to the high-rise metropolis of Bombay. These days, he has little time to admire the view. His cellular phone rings constantly as he gives instructions to his staff and clients, in between fielding calls from a venture capital fund that may take a stake in his software company.

Thirty-four-year-old Misra is now an Internet entrepreneur, running Starcom Software, an Internet solutions company servicing clients that include blue-chip Indian companies; institutions like India's National Stock Exchange and the National Securities Depository Ltd (India's record of share certificates); the Indian Express newspaper group; and the world's largest VSAT (very small aperture terminal) satellite project, promoted by the diversified business group, S Kumar.

Just five years ago, Misra's story would have been completely different. A graduate of the Indian Institute of Technology, Misra would probably have been standing in a queue outside the US consulate, seeking a visa to study at a top US university or, if he were luckier, to work in Silicon Valley. Many of his predecessors at India's six ITs – Bombay, Delhi, Kanpur, Kharagpur, Madras and Gauhati – did just that. Since their foundation in the late 1940s under Indian's first prime minister, Jawaharlal Nehru, many parents saw the IITs as the best way to equip their bright children with the skills that would win them exit to the West. Thousands apply each year; less than one per cent make it. IITgraduates are math-savvy class-toppers who formed the backbone of the research labs of US universities which granted them scholarships.

After graduation, US companies lapped them up. They personified the new economy, then emerging on the US west coast: they were flexible, intelligent, technology wizards, spoke English well and could easily cross boundaries and blend into cultures in pursuit of the big dream.

Indian engineers populated the high-tech companies of California, slogging long hours developing killer applications and smart codes, to make the world's computer systems hum efficiently and smoothly. They brought exceptional energy to the industry, and played an important role in the creation of the so-called dotcom economy, people like Venky Harinarayan, who sold his powerful e-commerce site, *junglee.com* for US$180 million, and Sabeer Bhatia, who raked in US$400 million dollars, selling his creation, the world's best-known email website, *hotmail.com*, to Microsoft. Anna Lee Saxenian, a professor of city and regional planning at the University of California at Berkeley, who studies Silicon Valley, says Indians, most of whom graduated from IITs, founded about ten per cent of the start-ups in Silicon Valley between 1995 and 1998. The brain drain over the past half-century has been massive. Enlightened Indian bureaucrats like N Vittal might argue, half in jest, that 'brain drain is better than brain in the drain', but there was a real social cost: 40–50% of IIT graduates went to the US every year, about 20,000 are believed to be in the US now, almost 20% of the total IIT population since the institutes were started. Most never returned.

They left India not only because of the opportunities the US offered, but because India at the time, in marked contrast to its open, pluralistic political system, placed innumerable bureaucratic and legal obstacles in the way of business and technical innovation. Importing technology, even critical software applications in export promotion zones, was difficult; profit and earnings were taxed at high rates; companies were penalised if they were efficient and produced more than their quotas; firms were prevented from exporting their products unless they completed tedious formalities. 'We were prevented from realising our potential,' says Arvind Agarwala, chief executive of Singapore-based Vedika Software, who moved to Singapore to set up his company and produced a successful branded accounting software package, FACT. 'We were never really free,' said Anand Mahindra, a leading executive with Mahindra and Mahindra, a jeep and tractors manufacturer. 'I never needed to plan, the government did it for us.'

But in 1988, when Misra completed his graduate degree from the

IIT, he decided to stay on in India, bucking the trend among his classmates. 'I suppose India was exciting enough at that time,' he says. In a sense it certainly was. In the mid–1980s, Texas Instruments overcame Indian bureaucratic hurdles and established a direct satellite link between its headquarters in the US and its research facility in the southern Indian city of Bangalore. Senior engineers at Texas Instruments found that a large part of its research and development team was from India – why not go to the source, they reasoned. Rajiv Gandhi, the prime minister at the time, was excited about computer technology and wanted a computer in every school in India. 'That decision by TI put Bangalore on the international map,' says Ashok Soota, a former president of Wipro group, one of India's leading integrated information technology companies.

Texas Instruments was followed by many more companies lured by the sylvan, wooded city on India's central plateau that Indians call an air-conditioned paradise. Army generals retire to Bangalore, the country's defence research industries are located there, as is the aircraft manufacturer Hindustan Aeronautics and other critical engineering companies. The prestigious Indian Institute of Science is based in Bangalore and it is an important centre of the movie industry.

Today, there are hundreds of top software companies in Bangalore. Some set up by multinationals, others by Indians returning after a successful stint in the US, others still by local entrepreneurs, who see, in information technology, a unique opportunity to catapult India into a global technological superpower.

Misra believes India can easily do it. In 1996, he decided to form his own business in Bombay, the country's financial capital, even though he knew it would be hard, and even though many of his classmates and friends were settling in exotic locations overseas. 'I didn't see any reason to go outside India and struggle in a society where I would have to learn to play golf and discuss baseball scores.' He started from a spare room in his apartment and, by the end of 2000, his firm will count 50 engineers and earnings of nearly US$5 million, up from about US$200,000 last year. Misra is considering setting up offices overseas but will maintain control from India.

Such an astonishing growth rate is hardly uncommon in India: the software industry grew 70% last year to over US$6 billion, up from 50% growth over the preceding year. India has at least 200,000 software

Bangalore, worker displaying circuit board – Credit: Chris Stowers/Panos

professionals, more than half of them women, and there is a demand for 55,000 more every year. The momentum this has created is leading to some reversal of the brain drain that at one point drew the best and brightest Indian minds overseas.

What has changed? Misra says it is easier access to capital. And the capital is coming his way not just from foreign-owned venture capital funds that are opening offices in India, nor from Indian banks or financial institutions. The common man, Misra says, is willing to bet on a business that has spawned this huge wave of optimism and is sending the shares of Indian infotech companies like Satyam, Infosys and Wipro to stratospheric heights and making their promoters phenomenally rich. 'We are bypassing the old government-created infrastructure of India,' Misra says. 'We are moving so fast the controls can't keep pace.'

And that, in turn, is changing the way Indians in Silicon Valley view their future. Some are returning to India and changing the corporate scene. They are passing work on to India – not just the dull, back-breaking code-maintenance work, but higher-end work, like development and design. From fixing bugs while the West slept to writing enormous, labour-intensive programmes, the industry has now leaped to the next stage of developing and designing systems. Leading the charge are companies like Satyam, Infosys and Wipro.

Consider Satyam, the Hyderabad-based company that made its name as a Y2K-buster. In 1999, it earned nearly 28% of its US$90m revenue from debugging the so-called Millennium Bug problem. Now it has moved beyond Y2K to set up India's largest private Internet service, with nearly 100,000 subscribers. When Satyam issued its depository receipts (as Indian shares are called in international markets) on NASDAQ, the preferred stock exchange for IT companies, its shares were initially offered at US$18; today their value exceeds US$100.

Or Infosys, a company formed by NR Narayana Murthy, a 53-year-old engineer, in Bangalore. He put the company together with seven partners and a pool of US$1,000 in 1981. Today, it provides Internet and e-commerce services to large western corporations and its shares are among the most sought-after on NASDAQ. Infosys employs 6,000 people, has a modern, 42-acre campus that looks as if it has been lifted out of California and pulls down annual revenues of Rs5 billion (US$122 million).

Wipro employs 6,500 people worldwide and earned US$310 million last year. It is capitalised at US$62 billion and its unassuming chairman, Azim Premji, is today the world's third richest person. It also makes personal computers. Unlike one-day wonders in the dotcom world, like World Online and *lastminute.com*, which have yet to show real profits, these are real, profitable companies, generating cash and growing each year by leaps and bounds.

The Internet – more accurately infotech – revolution has transformed the way India is perceived in the smarter set of western capitalism. No longer just a Christian Aid poster, it has moved from underdog to top dog in this area. But strength in high-tech industries alone won't allow India to fight the demographic reality that makes it an underdog. Every year, India's population grows by about 16 million. Economists have estimated that just to keep pace with the birth rate, India will have to add 127,000 schools, 373,000 schoolteachers, 2.5 million houses, 4 million jobs, 114,000 miles of cloth and 6 million tons of food each year.

But prosperity creates a middle class, and the middle classes demand good education. Literacy is the greatest antidote to overpopulation: the more literate parts of India, like the southern state of Kerala, have low, western-style birth rates.

Beyond that, the high-tech industry provides hope. It keeps talented, wealth-generating Indians like Misra in India, and has allowed smart Indian companies like Infosys to remain rooted in India while getting plugged into the new economy. Ignoring the controls, bypassing the hurdles that a bureaucratic India once placed on them, Indian information technology professionals are leaping over the barriers, making the world their plaything. ❏

Salil Tripathi, *a regular contributor to* Index, *is a writer based in London*

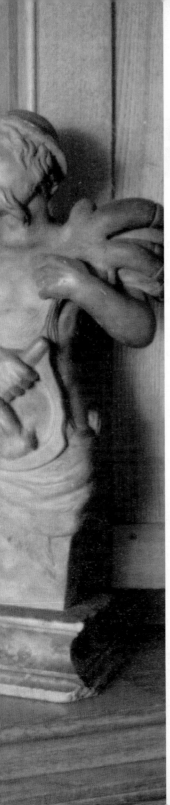

Culture

New fiction from China

Secrets of the British Museum

MOUNA NAIM

A poet goes to school

Mahmoud Darwish's verse has always been controversial, outraging the PLO, the Palestinian Authority and successive Israeli governments in equal measure. The reason for this outrage is Darwish's articulation of the experiences of a helpless people thrown out of their country and deprived of their right to determine their own destiny. 'We travel like other people' and other poems written after the Palestinian exodus from Beirut in 1982, for instance, offended many in the Palestinian diaspora when read for the first time in London in 1983; in Israel's case, offence was the rule rather than the exception.

Yasser Abed Rabbo, minister of culture and information in the Palestinian Authority, has just decided to publish an anthology of Israeli poetry. It's a neat riposte to the Israeli minister of education's recent proposal to include the poem *To My Mother* by Palestinian Mahmoud Darwish in a school anthology. Darwish thinks it an 'excellent idea', demonstrating that Palestinians 'have no complexes, an open mind and confidence in themselves and their culture'. 'As for myself,' the poet added, 'I'm always ready to meet Israeli intellectuals and poets.'

That was on 20 March. Only a few days earlier, it had taken a furious five-hour-long debate and a failed motion of censure against the government, to get the Knesset to agree to Yossi Sarid's proposal that Darwish's work would be included in Israeli school textbooks.

Darwish, one of the most important poets in the contemporary Arab world, is both an icon and the idol of the Palestinian diaspora. Twice he has been forced to leave his own country: the first time was with his parents in 1948 immediately following the declaration of the state of Israel; the second, two years later, when his parents tried to return from Lebanon. They found their village in Galilee had been razed to the ground to make way for an Israeli colony. The experience was instrumental in his early commitment to the Palestinian cause – which earned him three spells in Israeli prisons in the 1960s. In the 1970s, he joined the ranks of the Palestinians in exile, first in Cairo and later in Beirut. Until 1993, he was a member of the PLO's Executive Council, but resigned in that year to mark his disapproval of the Israeli-Palestinian accords concluded in Oslo. After living for some years in Paris, he now divides his time between Ramallah on the West Bank and Amman in Jordan.

'The Israeli decision is a big step forward in recognising the culture of the Other,' he said when interviewed in Paris towards the end of March. 'It's not an upheaval nor a revolution; it's just someone on the left who recognises that peace means Israeli society must open up to the Other, particularly to the Palestinian Other who lives alongside it on the same patch of ground. It's no more than the new Israeli historians, who acknowledge the injustice done to the Palestinians in the name of the creation of Israel, are saying (*Index* 3/95).'

Short of a ministerial crisis, 'Political discussion on my case is closed,' he says, 'but there is another debate, on the cultural front, about the Israeli's ability to admit that there is another people, with a common history, memories and feelings, rights and a deep attachment to the land the Zionists claimed was an empty desert up to their arrival, existing under Israeli rule.'

Those who are against Yossi Sarid's decision, he says, 'Fear that teaching my poems – a love song to the land and a celebration of an uninterrupted relationship with it – will push the younger generation to ask themselves questions. And then there is the problem of Israel's integration into the Near East: geographically it's part of the region but culturally it has always cut itself off.'

But now, according to Darwish, 'A breach has opened in the insurmountable wall of ignorance and denial of the Palestinian Other in Israel.' As far as he is concerned, knowledge of Palestinian culture is more about intelligence gathering and the poet Mahmoud Darwish is, in popular opinion, nothing more than 'a stereotype of absolute evil; the enemy'.

Views on Sarid's decision are divided: the majority of intellectuals held their tongues, but an opinion poll revealed that 37% of Israelis were in favour of the minister's initiative. And that's progress: while Hebrew translations of Darwish's poems have been around a considerable time, it was, as he says himself, largely in order to discover what the enemy was thinking about.

Things are beginning to change. The first translation of his latest collection, *The Bed of the Stranger*, was into Hebrew and the first edition was a sell-out. 'They are love poems,' he insists, 'and that demands a new way of reading, a literary approach.'

'Things are changing,' agrees the poet, 'but like all changes in Israel, it's happening with a certain amount of violence. Five hours debate in parliament on poetry! No poetry evening ever lasted that long.' ❑

Mouna Naïm *is Middle East corrrespondent for* Le Monde, *in which this article first appeared.*
Trsanslated by Judith Vidal-Hall

MAHMOUD DARWISH/ABDULLAH AL-UDHARI

The Truth Has Two Faces and the Snow Is Black

The truth has two faces and the snow is black over
    our city.
We can no longer despair more than our desperation, and the
End walks to the wall with confident steps
On the tiled floor wet with tears.
Who will bring down our flags: them or us?
King of the dying, who will read out 'The peace Accord'.
Everything's worked out for us beforehand. Who will remove
    our names
From our identity: you or them? Who will plant within us
The diaspora speech: 'We couldn't breakthrough the siege.
Let's hand in our paradise's keys to the minister of peace
    and save ourselves...'
The truth has two faces, our sacred slogan was a sword for us
And against us. What did you do with our castle before the
    light of this day?
You didn't fight because you feared martyrdom, but your
    throne is your coffin,
So carry your coffin to keep your throne.
King of waiting, this place will turn us into dust...
Who will bury our days after us: you...or them?
Who will raise their flags over our walls: you...or
    a desperate knight?
Who will hang their bells over our journey: you...or
    a desperate guard?
King of the dying, everything's worked out for us,
So why do you drag on with your negotiation?

We travel like Other People

We travel like other people, but we return to nowhere. As
    if travelling
Is the way of the clouds. We have buried our loved ones in
    the shadows of the clouds, between the roots of the trees.
And we said to our wives: go on giving birth to people like
    us for hundreds of years so we can complete this journey
To the hour of a country, to a metre of the impossible.
We travel in the carriages of the psalms, sleep in the tent
    of the prophets and come out of the speech of the gypsies.
We measure space with a hoopoe's beak or sing to while away
    the distance and cleanse the light of the moon.
Your path is long so dream of seven women to bear this long
    path
on your shoulders. Shake palm trees for them to know their
    names and who'll be the mother of the boy of Galilee.
We have a country of words. Speak speak so I can put my
    road on the stone of a stone.
We have a country of words. Speak speak so we may know the
end of this travel.

I talk too much

I talk too much about the insignificant difference between
    women and trees,
And the charm of the earth; about a coutnry whose stamp I
    could never find on the passport.
I ask: My good ladies and gentlemen, is the land of mankind
    for all mankind as you claim?
If so, where's my small hut and where am I? And the conference
    hall applauds me
For another three minutes, three minutes of independence and
    recognition...The conference has agreed
To our right to return, like all the hens and all the horses,
    to a stonedream.
I shake hands with each of them, then bow to them and go on
    travelling
To another country to babble about the difference between
    the mirage and the rain
And ask: My good ladies and gentlemen, is the land of
    mankind
For all mankind?

To My Mother

I long for my mother's bread
My mother's coffee
My mother's touch.
And the child within me grows up
Day by day
And I love my years because
When I die
I'd feel shy of my mother's tears.

If I return one day use me
As a veil for your eyelashes
And cover my bones with plants
Blessed by your untainted heels…
And tie my will
With one of your hair,
With a thread from the hem of your dress
So I can become a god,
Become a god
When I touch the bottom of your heart!

If I return one day use me
As fuel for your oven's fire,
As your roofterrace laundryline
Because I can no longer stand on my feet
Without your daylight prayers.
I have aged, give me back my childhood stars
So I can join the fledgling sparrows
On the return route
To your awaiting nest. ❏

Abdullah al-Udhari *is a poet and translator of Arab poetry. His most recent*
books are The Arab Creation Myth *and* Classical Poems by Arab Women

LAURA THOMAS

Eye of the beholder

A curator is trying to stop the break-up of a collection of erotica that illustrates one Victorian's magnificent obsession

When words fail, sometimes only a number will do. Area 51; Studio 54; Room 101 – tight-lipped digits that imply much and tell little. All have become synonymous with the sinister or the salacious. So it is with a cupboard in the British Museum's medieval and later antiquities department. Its contents were so profoundly shocking that for 135 years, access was strictly limited to gentlemen of 'taste and education'. This is Cupboard 55, the 'Secretum', hiding the scandalous legacy of a certain George Witt and still hidden from the general public.

Cupboard 55 does not reside in a dank basement or attic, but in a sunny corridor. The museum no longer enforces the strict visiting regulations that Witt imposed, allowing anyone who applies in writing to rifle through the remains of a very private pastime. Witt was no average Victorian amateur collector: he collected phalluses.

They are sculpted from stone, wax, amber, bronze, glass and, in most cases, have no body attached. Some have wings. One is decorated with small engraved birds and flowers that appear to be hanging from the foreskin. There's a cartoon depicting penises sitting in church pews, heads reverently bowed. Here is a medieval drinking vessel in the shape of a phallus; a collection of 19th-century Japanese pornographic cards; a copy of Giulio Romano's *Il Modi* (a kind of 16th-century good sex guide); pornographic scribblings by Fuseli; an 1840s edition of the catalogue from the Secretum in Naples; detailed scrapbooks of erotica from Pompeii and Herculaneum.

The array of objects is overwhelming, yet Dr David Gaimster, keeper of medieval and later antiquities, describes the contents of 55 as a

The Secretum, British Museum — Credit: Cinta Tumie

'residue'. Approximately half of Witt's collection – including classical figure vases and Indian temple reliefs – has since been removed and placed in other exhibitions within the museum.

To understand the artefacts, one has to think back to Chaucer and Boccaccio. The problem, Gaimster explains, is that most of the time we can't. His diagnosis is of a nasty case of 'Victoriavision': 'We tend to see the material through a very Victorian eye,' he says. It seems that at some point in the 19th century, we lost any sense of humour where winged penises were concerned – and the lapse persists. Many of the medieval and classical pieces are amulets, good-luck charms, fertility symbols, humorous and subversive in a *Carry-On* sort of way, but likely to have made John Ruskin blush. The shadows cast by such luminaries of the Victorian cultural landscape are long enough to leave us in the dark when it comes to appreciating the more eccentric elements of the Witt collection.

What, then, drove Witt to collect and hoard items he could never display in decent society? With only the scantiest of biographies – mainly pieced together from public records – that question has never been adequately answered. He was born in Norfolk in 1803 and studied medicine at Leiden in the 1830s. Success came early. He became the director of Bedford Infirmary in his 30s, then a fellow of the Royal Society, before being elected Mayor of Bedford in 1834. In fact, precisely the pillar of society one expects not to be fascinated by winged penises. For reasons unknown, he tired of England in the 1840s and headed to Australia. There, again for reasons unknown, he abandoned medicine to make a fortune from banking. A decade later, he returned to England and established a circle of gentlemen scholars preoccupied with items of 'phallic worship'.

Questions as to Witt's reasons for leaving England and medicine loom large. Did some professional gaffe necessitate a sudden departure? Much of his correspondence appears to have disappeared with him; we are left with Witt's public self, an empty, if eminent, husk of a man. We do know that through his discreet little club, Witt could acquire whatever objects he pleased. Gaimster points out that the collection tells us far more about the Victorian mind than it does about its collector, or even the antiquities contained within it. 'It tells us how 19th century scholars understood their world – and misunderstood a lot of it.' One of the more curious items in this category is what Witt believed to be a medieval chastity belt. An intimidating object with vicious metal teeth, it is, in fact, a fake, manufactured by Victorians for Victorians. 'I think Witt believed it was the real thing,' says Gaimster. 'This is how the Victorians imagined the medieval past.' He acknowledges 'an erotic tension' running through the collection that makes it more difficult to interpret. 'If we could be sure it was entirely scholarly, that would be one thing, but there are such contradictions in the material.' Leafing through the scrapbooks with their detailed illustrations of statues and frescoes, we come upon a section of photographs. Scantily clad women, dressed as gladiators, fight each other in a series of episodes designed to arouse more than scholarly attention.

It is in the shadowy area where archaeological and erotic interest meet that the key to Witt's obsession lies. The objects seem bizarre because of their collector's fixation with obscenity. He did not care to place them in any cultural or chronological milieu, where they would have been absorbed into the wider context alongside more everyday artefacts. Regardless of provenance – Pompeii, Herculaneum, Europe or the Far East – Witt selected the pieces by virtue of their obscenity value alone. The resulting legacy documents the Victorian encounter with the classical world and the farthest reaches of the British Empire.

It was not an entirely happy meeting: Gaimster calls it 'a major trauma'. 'The Roman world that was being discovered in Italy frequently depicted private life in its art.' Similar problems applied to discoveries in India and the Far East: 'The problem there was that heaven was depicted as a highly sexualised place. The Victorian idea of heaven was entirely chaste.' One only has to look at the British Museum to recognise that Victorian thought idealised the classical world as a civic and imperial model. Frescoes where frolicking satyrs, bestiality and orgies are commonplace, ran counter to this vision of order and restraint. The collapse of the Roman and Greek empires seemed to underline the notion that there was a concrete link between sexual excess and social disintegration.

If Witt and his colleagues were disturbed by what they found, why go to the trouble and expense of shipping it back to England? A pamphlet, published by Witt to mark the acceptance of his collection by the British Museum in 1865, is telling. Entwined with his obsession was a desire to legitimise his preoccupation. What could be more respectable than official acceptance by the British Museum? The museum's trustees, under director Anthony Panizzi, had 'no hesitation' in accepting a bequest 'of such quality', Gaimster says. The grey area of the erotic was transformed into the black and white of archaeological respectability, giving Witt's secret passion the rubber stamp of high cultural approval. Naturally, provision was made for the protection of the morally suggestible in contemporary society. Witt insisted the collection be allotted a room where it could be viewed – for scholarly purposes – by men of an appropriate education and class. In a final example of the contradictions of the man, Witt censored his life's secret work.

Dr Gaimster is determined to prevent any further break-up of the collection. He argues that it is a 'time capsule, a laboratory' for studying the way the Victorians made sense of history. He plans to use Witt's collection as the centrepiece of an exhibition on the 'censorship of

The Secretum, British Museum – Credit: Gina Turner

antiquity'. By 2003, the Mayor of Bedford's best-kept secret may be on display in all its glory. The modest approbation Witt gained for his curious pastime will be eclipsed in a blaze of prurient publicity. It's probably not what he would have wanted. ❏

Laura Thomas *works for the BBC Social Affairs Unit*

YO YO

The function of bathing

Whenever Xiezi walked along beside her fatther the mingled stench of stale urine and the odour of a man's body unwashed for a very long time wafted across her nostrils. Xiezi's father had always clung to his peasant origins. Despite taking part in the revolution and being head of a factory, the muck from his time in the Eighth 'Dirt' Route Army fighting the Japanese still clung to him, ingrained and unwashable.

Xiezi's father was deeply repulsed by the thought of bathing and passionately believed it could bring about all manner of evils. He would say: 'See those youngsters all pink and shiny like fucking scrubbed-up piglets, they're just showing off and doing their best to stir up a hornets' nest for the rest of us. Have a few washes and before you know what den of demons you've pissed on, you're divorced, your home and money are gone, floozies under the bed and all because of washing!'

He had yet more irrefutable evidence against washing: wasn't it with an army of unwashed peasants that the Great Leader Chairman Mao had beaten that bald western lackey Chiang Kai-shek and chased him off to his tiny little island. 'It was that dickhead Chiang who told his armies to wash whenever they could, the pussies, that turned them into the bunch of panda pups we Communists battered to a pulp!'

But Xiezi's father had another unmentionable terror of water. The thought of washing forced him to recall his three sons who had drowned in the river many years before. Water was their family demon. Water had executed their family's heirs. Despite being a devout Marxist, an atheist who refused to subjugate himself to destiny and a highly principled Communist, Xiezi's father clung to this one unshakeable superstition.

Xiezi's father's factory gave out tickets for the public bathhouse as a kind of welfare benefit; if the date on them expired before use, tough. So, once a fortnight, Xiezi would take her sisters to the bathhouse. With

Hainan Island, China, demolished house – Credit: Catherine Platt/Panos

so many days' grime it was as though their bodies were actually heavier with dirt. The bright cleanliness they felt after bathing was unimaginable before the event and Xiezi always felt as though swallows had returned to their forests on the first days of spring: lithe and happy. Bathing, especially in winter when it was particularly treasured, was more or less the highlight of their monotonous lives in that city of swirling dust and choking fumes where some of the city folk only rarely enjoyed the privilege, once a month or even less. Each time she bathed, Xiezi was surprised to discover how much whiter she and her sisters were.

On one cold winter's day, Xiezi took her little column of sisters to the bathhouse as usual. She stood beneath the hot streaming water allowing it to course in rivulets down the contours of her body to her toes. She looked at her breasts, swelling larger each day, and felt a twinge of shyness she could not explain. Her arms and legs were long and slender and her skin shone a soft olive, seldom seen among people from these cold northern climes. It glowed bright as a bronze urn, but people did not admire or appreciate it. Round here there is a saying: 'A touch of white hides all flaws.' Indeed, it was because of her skin colour that people said she was unattractive – in some eyes even a little strange.

Standing in the midst of all these naked women she quietly and unconsciously examined the physique of each person: the old, the young, the fat and the thin, the smooth and shiny and the rough and coarse, big bums, small bums, thin and thick waists, long and short legs, barrel bodies and slender waifs, pert little breasts, great sagging bosoms. She looked again at her own delicately turned-up breasts and felt for the first time in her life a soft rush of arousal. She had never imagined her own body could be beautiful, unflawed and she admired herself as though appreciating a pearl. The smells of the countless bodies mingling with the heady perfume of cheap soap threatened suffocation, but the women, damp in the steam, paid no heed as they scrubbed each other's backs and laughed at each other's jokes. Xiezi heard middle-aged women talking about things that made her blush bright red; others slowly ambled here and there, visiting, natural and grand as trees, with not the slightest sign of shyness in their nudity.

Xiezi found herself closing her eyes and putting back her head to let the gushing water caress her face and soak away the collected filth and tiredness of so many days. Soon, forgetting where she was, she felt a contentedness she had never imagined. The water spread like a veil from heaven across her eyes and she seemed to be floating on air.

In the depth of her steam-induced reverie, Xiezi suddenly sensed with shock a pair of eyes, man's eyes, looking directly at her! Horrified by the maleness of the gaze, she automatically covered the most secret part of her body with both hands. There was a framed photograph of the Great Leader hanging high on the wall of the showers. He was smiling slightly through the rolling steam at the naked women below, solemn, amiable; and in his perceptive and benevolent gaze was an infinite mercy and compassion. Xiezi was suddenly breathless and her whole body tensed. She knew it was impossible to walk through the bathing house with the same insouciance of a moment before. She felt like a thief, startled yet unable to run. Gingerly, she tiptoed through the bathhouse, hiding herself and unable to raise her eyes, her movements embarrassed and prudish. She dressed herself with trembling hands and quickly left the building, abandoning her sisters. But even as she fled through the door she could still feel those eyes scrutinising her from behind.

She stood in the street gulping breaths of air, her heart gripped with terror. The sky was like lead, the air thick with choking coal smoke: as every winter, thick coils of acrid smoke rose from every home. Xiezi stood in the street, swathed in smog and shaking with fear. What was so fearsome in those eyes? She dare not admit it even to herself.

Because of those eyes, she went less frequently to the bathhouse. When her body itched more than she could endure, she would draw a basin of water and, while everyone slept, quietly scrub herself down behind her door, still afraid of those ubiquitous eyes.

As the weather got warmer, she occasionally caught a whiff of her own unpleasant odour, enough sometimes to make her gag. Whenever she drew water to wash, her mother chided her saying: 'What're the washhouse tickets for? Why do you want to waste our water?' In the face of such reprimands, Xiezi's quandary grew even more intractable.

One evening, while snow flakes as big as goose feathers slowly fell outside, Xiezi, who had just cleared away after the family meal, went into the main room where her mother was sewing cotton shoes by the gloom of a 15-watt bulb. She silently crossed the floor to her mother's side and started gently massaging her feet. Idly, her eyes cast round the empty walls of the room – blank except for a huge poster of 'Chairman Mao Going to An Yuan'. Xiezi looked up at his divine image and a shudder went down her spine.

'Ma,' she asked, her voice barely above a whisper, 'what do you reckon to that portrait of our Great Leader Chairman Mao in the bathhouse?' Her mother shot up in her seat and stared, surprised.

'It's good, of course. The light from Chairman Mao shines in all directions; the light from Chairman Mao brightens every corner,' she recited. Then she paused and, as though suddenly remembering something, she fixed a stare on Xiezi. 'Why are you asking me that? You looking to die?' She paused again and released a long, slow sigh. 'Never ever talk like that outside these walls. And don't go asking stupid questions – all that stuff is out of bounds.' So saying, she softly stroked her daughter's hair. 'Now get yourself off to bed, okay?'

This was the first time her mother had touched her since the death of her three sons.

When Xiezi got up at dawn the next day, she crawled under her bed and groped around until she found a small earthenware jar. She brought it out and lightly brushed away a thin layer of dust. She hesitated a moment then thrust her hand in and drew out a small package, tightly rolled in brown straw-paper, itself matted with dust. She unwrapped it layer by layer with all the care of someone uncovering priceless treasures in gold and jade. She removed the last piece of wrapping and there before her were some banknotes. The largest was two jiao, there were three one-jiao notes and an assortment of smaller one- and two-fen notes. Xiezi spread the money out before her and counted a total of nine jiao, three fen. This was the sum of four years' saving, four years of scrimping and sacrifices; it was the only thing in her life that was entirely hers.

But today she bundled it up without thinking and stuffed it into her pocket. She crunched through the snow and whistling wind to the Xinhua bookshop. Blinkered and determined she let go of four years' savings like a pent-up breath and got in exchange four larger-than-life-size colour portraits of Chairman Mao.

She had one fen left in her pocket.

When the teller had rolled up the portraits and placed them in Xiezi's hand, she felt her soul shine with a divine light. Carefully and reverentially she tucked them away next to her heart, not wanting the weather to taint such sacred treasures. She opened the door of the shop and stepped out to face the wind and driving snow. Unconcerned by the bitter cold she walked home cradling in her bosom this great spiritual sustenance, and she felt comfort and solace in her repentance.

So, to become accustomed to those eyes, she hung the four portraits of Chairman Mao over her and her sisters' beds. Every day, eight sacred eyes watched her, yet still she had to hide behind the bed when she changed her underwear. She was deeply enraged by her own timidity, and forced herself to expose her secret before those sacred eyes. She deliberately lay naked on her bed letting the 'light that shines in all directions, the light that brightens every corner' fall upon her body. She stripped off once, twice, again and again before that holy gaze to try and steel her body against this shyness. But she just felt more and more uncomfortable before his eyes and more and more she wanted to do something shocking and unforgivable.

To punish herself yet further, Xiezi decided to get to school at six o'clock every morning to light the stove in her classroom and sweep the floor. In the depths of those winter months when she woke at five in the morning the sky was still pitch black. Fierce cold accompanied the silence of dawn. Xiezi would reluctantly drag herself from the warmth of her bedding but as soon as she remembered the slogan 'Reform your thinking through labour', she would fling open the door and march through the bitter cold to school. By the time it was light, every day throughout the winter, the classroom had been swept clean.

Every Saturday afternoon there was a clear-out at school, and Xiezi would stand on tiptoes, on top of a stool, on top of her desk and, reaching high above her head, take down the portrait of Chairman Mao hanging in the middle of the classroom. Xiezi had a problem with heights and when she was up there her legs would tremble. But if she was going to show her devotion to Chairman Mao, she would have to overcome this small difficulty. When she had the portrait before her in her hands, she gazed once again into those eyes, and reverentially wiped his image clean. Solemnly she wiped the dust from the frame, then, finally, ritually hung it back in its place. Everyone present was deeply moved by her devotion and, at the end of term, of all the Red Guards Xiezi was judged to have the most limitless devotion to the Great Leader Chairman Mao. ❑

Yo Yo *left China 11 years ago and is now based in London. The above is excerpted from her new novel,* The Spirit of the Tide, *currently being translated*
This excerpt translated by Ben Carrdus

BRICE FLEUTIAUX

Missing in action

Credit: Enki Bilal

Brice Fleutiaux, 33, a French freelance photographer, has been held hostage in Chechnya since early October 1999. He was apparently kidnapped in the Grozny suburbs while on his way to the office of President Aslan Mashkadov to ask for protection.

On 31 October, the Russian security services released a video and a text in which Fleutiaux writes: 'I am in a cellar with no windows, light or electricity … I am treated like a dog, like an animal. They come at any hour and wake me. They're completely drunk. They think they can do what they want with me.'

Since then, two notes written in November and January have been passed to his family; a second video, released in mid-December, was sent to the French security services. Chechen rebels said in January that Fleutiaux was free but unable to leave Chechnya because of the continuing fighting. There has been no further news since then.

The French foreign ministry raised the case with Vladimir Putin in November. Unlike the Babitsky affair (*Index* 2/00), media response has been poor and press freedom organisations have only recently turned their attention to Fleutiaux's situation.

Born in Toulouse in 1967, Fleutiaux began his career in Cambodia in 1989. He later worked in India, Bangladesh, Vietnam and former Yugoslavia. ❏

An exhibition of Brice Fleutiaux's photographs is at the Freedom Forum, Stanhope Place, London W2, from 2 – 31 May. His support committee can be found at http//fleutiaux.brice.free.fr

Cambodia, 1992

Khmer refugee camp, Thailand, 1989

Ambush, Croatia, 1991

Barasti, Romania, 1996

BABEL

Talking Chinese

*T*he highly visible base of the Chinese in Britain, in the form of their
restaurants and fast-food outlets, belies the near invisibility of the community
itself. Those who run the restaurants work night and day, seven days a week;
only the waiters learn English and then only as much as they need to do the job.
The community is not concentrated in any one town or region, and has little time
to set up community associations, or lobby on their own behalf. Nor, unlike other
immigrant communities, are they linked by ready-made religious institutions;
religion is a family affair largely concerned with appeasing the ancestors.

The women, in particular, are cut off from the host community. Many never
work in the restaurants but stay at home looking after children or grandchildren;
many grannies, as in the cases below, have been brought over in later life for
precisely that purpose. They have no chance to learn English, let alone adapt to
English society and its strange cuisine. Their problems are compounded by age
when, with the breakdown of the extended family, many are abandoned to their
fate. The case of Mrs Wong is quite atypical. There is little provision for them in
the host community: sheltered housing schemes such as that below are rare and, in
this case at least, happened almost incidentally.

This is a community hiding behind its stoicism and unwillingness to complain
– even when communication is possible. Mrs Lee No 1, for instance, was chosen
to talk to me because her community worker saw her as cheerful and
communicative; he had no idea that she had been abandoned by most of her
children and grandchildren, or of the pain this caused her. Tales of neglect and of
literal abandonment abound.

All the women here are from Hong Kong not from the Cantonese-speaking
cities, however, but from the rural New Territory where they were small farmers
living in extended family compounds. The isolation they encounter in Britain
feels especially acute. Their families operate the lower end of the Chinese catering
business – takeaways and fish-and-chip shops.

NICK MORETON, SENIOR EXECUTIVE OF TRIDENT HOUSING ASSOCIATION WHICH FUNDS AND RUNS CONNAUGHT GARDENS AND CHERISH HOUSE:

The first I knew about this project was during a funding round when I found that all the projects we'd suggested were deleted, but there was a million pound (US$1.6m) grant towards housing aged Chinese. We didn't do any elaborate research. We built Connaught Gardens with some Chinese detail in the façade, but it could have been used for anything if the community hadn't wanted to make use of it. Then we sent flyers round the Chinese takeaways and waited to see what would happen. And they came out of the woodwork, just like that.

MARGARET TAN, PROJECT MANAGER OF CHERISH HOUSE:

The Chinese don't make a fuss or demand anything. They are the hidden race. And when they get old, access to public and social services is denied them because of their lack of English and their frailty. They can't get to the doctor, to the police. They can't ring 999 because they only speak Chinese. I wanted to get some social service information in Chinese, but though they had the information in Bengali, Hindi, Urdu, they didn't have it in Chinese. I sent one of our residents to hospital once, and straightaway the hospital rang me and asked why did you send this person, what can we do, she only speaks Chinese. One resident was in hospital and discharged himself after a few days because he couldn't eat anything; he'd never eaten English food and no Chinese food was provided.

Their children, the next-generation Chinese, aren't interested in leisure the way the British are. They are just interested in money and status and cars. So they see the old people as a hindrance – they don't speak English, they are in the way. There are some terrible cases of old people being dumped on the steps of churches.

MRS LEE NO 1 (76):

I've nine grandsons and granddaughters. All of them are in England. They very seldom come here. I came here 26 years ago when I was 51 years old. My husband was working here already, so I followed with our sons and daughters. He was working in a Chinese takeaway, but I was busy looking after the children, I didn't work. I looked after the first grandchild too. I babysat and sometimes I cooked *congee* for him and the other babies. But I don't see him now. He never comes to see me. I played with him when he was little but now he forgets me, he doesn't come. He's getting towards the end of school already, I don't know exactly how old he is. I don't know the ages of the youngest grandchildren – they don't live in Birmingham but far away; I don't know the names of the cities. Though my eldest grandson speaks Chinese, many of the others don't. Their idea of Chinese culture is a Chinese takeaway. But they still look like Chinese people. What's the point of feeling happy or sad about it, I can't do anything about it.

When I was a child, my grandmother lived in the same house as I did and my mother too. It's different now. Chinese families all used to live together, but not any more. It's better that old way. The grandmother can help take care of the grandchildren.

No, I wasn't surprised to see the British live so differently. That's no business of mine. But I think the British grandmother likes her grandchildren more than we like ours.

MRS LEE NO 2 (67):

My children come here to see me very frequently. They bring our grandsons and granddaughters to see my husband and me. A few years ago, I used to help look after the children. But they all go to school now. The eldest is seven years old, the youngest about three. These days I go shopping with them. I buy things for them. And when they come to my house I cook for them. I don't sing songs or tell stories, we don't do that. My sons and sons-in-law are all working in takeaways. My daughters and daughters-in-law look after the house and the children. Sometimes I visit their homes. More often, when they have all finished work, they come and take me to the restaurant. I see them and my grandchildren more than most people see their children and grandchildren. I'm lucky.

I'm used to the cold here now. Now, when I go back to Hong Kong, I feel too hot.

MRS WONG (C70):

I've spent 26 years in England. My first husband was much older than me. It was a marriage made by a matchmaker. He came here nine years before me, but he was useless. He liked drinking, and gave me very little money. I even had to borrow money for the plane fare. I left my children

in Hong Kong with my mother, and when I'd found work I went back
to Hong Kong to fetch them, I arrived here with the children and
baggage and no money. I had to work very hard to earn it all myself
because my husband didn't. He died in 1987.

I have only one grandchild from my eldest daughter but I haven't
seen him for a couple of years. I always remember him. He is 14 or 15
years old now and disabled. I looked after him for seven years, I never
closed my eyes looking after him while his mother was working. But

then I hurt my back and I can't do it any more, and now my daughter won't speak to me. She is very bitter because when she left school I didn't have the money for her to go to university, she had to work in a takeaway like me. It's very difficult. But for my other three children, I'd be crying all the time.

The other children love me because they know how hard I worked for them. I worked all over – Swansea, then Epsom and Carshalton. We lived in a run-down council house. The eldest son had to cook for the youngest children. I got time off when I could to be with them, but my next-door neighbour, an Englishwoman, looked in to see if they were all right. And the next-door neighbours helped us do up the house too. They were kind. These friends still send us cards. I think English people are very courteous.

All my younger children went to university. They studied computers. My younger daughter went to San Francisco two years ago to work with computers. She rings me every week on a Saturday and speaks to me for a least half an hour. I'm going to visit her in San Francisco next year. She's not married yet. I have a son in Bristol and another in London, both of them work in computers too and live with their girlfriends. The one in London's girlfriend is English. She's learning to cook Chinese food, but I don't teach her. She's learning it out of a book.

When I wanted to get married again, I asked my children's permission. My second husband had five children, all born here. They're very western, they don't care about us. When they do come, the grandchildren are so innocent, they say 'bye-bye, grandma' and 'give us a kiss' in English, they don't speak any Chinese and they don't realise we can't understand. My husband can't speak to them at all, and not much to his children. His son does speak broken Hakka but it's not enough. Once, I cooked a great meal for everyone and no one came because there was a confusion of dates: they hadn't understood each other.

Even my sons I have to remind about Chinese festivals, the New Year and so forth, when they are coming up. They wouldn't know otherwise. My daughter in San Francisco is better, there is much more of a Chinese community there, she speaks Chinese all the time.

MRS CHENG (86):
I have three granddaughters and three grandsons. The eldest is 26 or 27; the youngest 18. They visit me whenever they've got time. They can

speak Hakka, but mostly they speak English. They don't usually eat meals at my house. But sometimes – once or twice a year – they take me to a restaurant. I've lived here since 1991. I didn't know anyone here before, but I have friends now.

I've been in England 26 years. I came when I was 60, after my husband died. My son – he's 61 now and retired – had a fish-and-chip shop, he brought me over. I lived alone then, over the fish-and-chip shop. He and his family lived elsewhere. It was lonely but what could I do about it. He only comes occasionally now. My friends' sons and daughters come to see them more often than he comes to see me.

We lived differently in Hong Kong. I was sent away from my family when I was 100 days old to live with my husband's family – that had all been arranged. He was three years older than me. We played together like brother and sister and I was brought up by my husband's grandmother. She loved me very much and treated me as a daughter. Traditionally, you got married at 20 and so we did. Things were all very formal at that time. He died when he was 60.

MRS WONG:

We don't know anyone outside here apart from our families. Our families wouldn't ask us to live with them. We're lucky to have friends here. And no, we don't really celebrate the festivals together. Maybe we cook more food.

MRS CHENG:

Our grandchildren understand more about British culture, British festivals than they understand about ours. We wish they did know more. But since they live here in England, we cannot compel then. They don't know any Chinese characters. They can't read Chinese. But then I can't read Chinese either.

MRS LEE NO 1:

I like it here at Connaught Gardens. I have friends and we play cards every day. ❏

Penelope Farmer, who conducted the interviews, is a writer. Her latest book is Sisters *(Viking, 1999)*
Interpreters: Wai-Ling Bickerton and Raymond Wong

Support for

It is the generosity of our friends and supporters which makes *Index on Censorship's* work possible. *Index* remains the only international publication devoted to the promotions and protection of that basic yet still abused human right, freedom of expression.

Your support is needed more than ever now as *Index* and the Writers & Scholars Educational Trust continue to grow and develop new projects. Donations help directly towards such work as the expansion of our website, which will make access to *Index's* stories and communication between free-speech activists and supporters even easier, and the education programme, which will see *Index* fostering a better understanding of censorship and anti-censorship issues in schools.

Please help *Index* speak out.

The Trustees and Directors would like to thank the many individuals and organisations who support *Index on Censorship* and Writers & Scholars Educational Trust, including:

If you would like more information about *Index on Censorship* or would like to support our work, please contact Hugo Grieve, Fundraising Manager, on (44) 20 7278 2313 or email hugo@indexoncensorship.org

Stand

BRITAIN'S FOREMOST LITERARY QUARTERLY

EDITORS

Michael Hulse
Kinsella

EDITORIAL OFFICE

School of English
University of Leeds
Leeds LS2 9JT
UK

+44 (0) 113 233 4794
+44 (0) 113 233 4791

EMAIL:
nd@english.novell.leeds.ac.uk

WEBSITE:
http://saturn.vcu.edu/~dlatane/stand.html

SUBSCRIPTIONS AND COMPETITIONS

Linda Goldsmith
Whistle House
George Street
Newcastle upon Tyne NE4 7JL
UK

+44 (0) 191 273 3280
+44 (0) 191 273 0555

SUBSCRIPTION RATES

One Year: £25.00 (UK and Europe)
£31.00/US$49.50 overseas)
Student/Unwaged: £18.00
19.00/US$30.00)
Single copy (by mail): £7.00
8.00/US$13.00)

IN THE JUNE 2000 ISSUE

NEW WRITING FROM AMERICA

Prose from Robert Coover, William Gass and Tama Janowitz, and poetry from John Hollander, Sharon Olds, Mary Jo Salter and Charles Simic.

PLUS

Hans Magnus Enzensberger, Hella S. Haasse, Tanure Ojaide, new translations of Chekhov, Horace and Leopardi, Marjorie Perloff on Emily Dickinson, Frank Kermode on Tony Tanner, C.K. Stead on Robert Gray and Andrew Biswell on W.G. Sebald.

"IF YOU WANT THE EXCITEMENT OF ORIGINAL LITERARY ACHIEVEMENT, OF A PASSION FOR IT, I RECOMMEND *STAND*."

RICHARD HOLMES

YANG LIAN

Leaving the 20th century

22**Dec 1999**: We fly into the new Beijing Capital Airport for the first time. Its silvery-grey 1990s-style building is in striking contrast to the older 1970s buildings, but the familiar 'long dragon' is still there: too few passport control points in customs, hundreds of Chinese and foreign passengers waiting in line.

Leaving the airport, the sky is bright blue and the distant hills clear and distinct, just as I remember a typical Beijing winter's day. But the taxi driver told us there had been a strong wind the previous few days that had blown away the pollution and, because of the millennium, some of the more heavily polluting factories had been ordered to halt production temporarily to preserve the views for the new year celebrations. 'Usually, there's a thick grey smog all day,' he says.

At night I need two duvets. I've forgotten how feeble the heating is in Beijing homes.

23 Dec 1999: Twelve degrees below zero. This, I hear, is the coldest day in Beijing for 20 years …

Compared with the last time I came here, Beijing is much cleaner and more spacious. I heard that because of celebrating the fiftieth National Day since the founding of the state, many engineering projects were finally brought to completion. The areas around Wang Fujing and Tiananmen have all been relaid with granite flagstones (some people say they saw sanitation workers using big vacuum cleaners). But walking through the streets of Beijing, this ancient city is already completely unrecognisable. Its buildings, apart from those inhabited by the nouveau riche, are utterly without taste or style. I suddenly thought, only an autocratic society can at a stroke so 'decide' to change an entire city's appearance.

Officially, the total spent nationwide on projects for the fiftieth National Day is 900 billion renminbi (RMB) (US $11 billion), 90% of the country's entire annual tax revenue of one trillion RMB spent on an official celebration! Unimaginable in the West! Will taxpayers ever put these two figures together?

24 Dec 1999: In the morning, we are picked up by Ms 'L', a freelance writer I met during my last return to China. She has just published a prose collection, *Melancholy of the Western Regions*, in the *New Youth Collection,* one of five books by writers born in the 1960s ... This whole set of books was brought into being, from commissioning through to the purchase of the publication number and printing, by Mr 'S', an independent literary merchant.

Ms 'L' hopes Yo Yo will give her next novel for publication to Mr 'S'.

Compared to the blatant exploitation by the state, this would be good for Yo Yo, at least financially. ...

25 Dec 1999: We spent the morning with Ms 'W', looking round her impressive factory in Tong County. Ms 'W' owns a fashion house, Mu Zhen Liao, which has cleverly renewed the language of traditional Chinese clothing and in the three years since starting up is already one of China's most successful clothing brand names. In the afternoon, at an exclusive Mu Zhen Liao display counter in Beijing's Yansha Shopping City, we saw Mu Zhen Liao clothes for around 500 RMB a piece, and shoppers falling over each other to buy them. I heard that on the first day of the marketing display, turnover came to more than 60,000 RMB. What I don't understand is that these clothes obviously exceed the levels of the general standard of living – even a German reporter who bought a sleeveless evening dress said 'I can't find an opportunity to wear it!' So where are China's white-collar workers going to wear it?

26 Dec 1999: The publisher Mr 'T', the literary merchant Mr 'S' and the writer Ms 'L' came to discuss Yo Yo's novel. Mr 'S' is from Xi'an and despite his honest, naive appearance, has a good command of the publishing business. Because he was not familiar with Yo Yo's work, his inquiries were very detailed, especially on the topics: a) Is the novel a good read? (ie, is it readable and directly relevant to the market) and b) Will it stir up official trouble or not?

Publication numbers are still controlled by a state system, but state publishing houses can sell their numbers on to private literary merchants, thereby 'creating income'. A normal price for a registration number is around 15,000 RMB whether it applies to one book only or a set. To keep costs down, therefore, merchants much prefer to publish sets. Once the book is out, the literary merchant arranges for reviews to appear in the press; critics who are not friends will demand 1,000 RMB per review. But it is the state publishing house that takes the flak if any of the books published 'in its name' create problems. If there is trouble with a book – at worst banning followed by public criticism – the publishing house can be shut down for rectification and the leadership changed; in less serious cases there would be a reduction in its allocation of publication numbers, amounting to a reduction in turnover and economic sanction. Additionally, the co-operation between literary merchant and publishing house would cease – a situation both parties do all they can to avoid. Consequently, when Mr 'S' heard of a detail in Yo Yo's novel during the Cultural Revolution when a girl has feelings of sexual revulsion towards a portrait of Chairman Mao in a public bath, he paid special attention. He felt that although this was a good selling point (sex and politics), it might cause problems and insisted on reading the whole manuscript before making a final decision (p166).

27 Dec 1999: Ms 'L' came to meet us and we drove to the Guolin Feng Bookshop in Hai Dian for the launch of *New Youth Collection*. Intensive launch ceremonies such as this with their attendant media hype were very popular for a while, but when every book began getting the same treatment, it became less effective and the method – known as 'stir-frying' – fell out of favour. However, because Guolin Feng is a famous, privately run cultural bookshop in Beijing, next to Beijing University with its intellectualised and serious readership, and because the book's title includes *New Youth*, directly evoking people's memories of every student intellectual movement since 'May Fourth' [The May Fourth Movement of 1919, sparked by China's unfair treatment in the Treaty of Versailles, sought to reinvent China in a modernised, western image. *Tr*], including, of course, June Fourth, the shop was heaving.

When we arrived, there were already some two hundred people surrounding a long table in the bookshop. The launch is being hosted by the editor of the magazine *Method*, which was famous for its liberal thinking but is now under orders to 'temporarily suspend publication'.

I was asked to kick off proceedings by introducing *Melancholy of the Western Regions*. The speakers after me were all famous liberal intellectuals in China, many of whom showed great courage in openly expressing their views in the recent debate on 'liberalism' and 'the new left'. Mr 'R' from Beijing University stood up and criticised one of the writers in the collection, Yu Jie, for writing forewords to other people's books, because 'It's so stupid only Li Peng would do it!' He spoke of Falun Gong: 'I am not a member of Falun Gong, but I will defend people's rights to freedom of belief.' With reference to the extravagance of the government's spending for the fiftieth National Day celebrations: 'That money belonged to laid-off workers!' With each point made, there was thunderous applause from the audience. I listened in a daze, wondering where I was!

As I left Guolin Feng the impassioned words were still ringing in my ears. But I walked away through the tide of people on the street, I felt the general level of apathy and indifference seemed twice as bad compared with what had just happened. Can it be that the Chinese government is genuinely accommodating more voices, or is this in actual fact just a gesture, an intellectual wank, an outpouring of words to hide the inadequacy of their actions? Who can answer?

Dec 28 1999: In the morning, the *Chinese News Week* reporter 'J' came for an interview. This magazine is quite interesting. The print quality is very high with a great deal of attention paid to the photographs and text. Each edition is divided into a section on politics, a section on culture and a special editorial. The special editorial in the last edition was about a batch of fake new-issue 100 RMB notes almost appearing at the same time as a genuine batch. But a close inspection of the political pages between their attractive covers shows the content is still bound by official strictures. It seems the Chinese *Time* magazine they want to produce is still a long way away.

In the afternoon I went to Hongqiao Beili to visit the old writers 'Y' and 'K'. Just before leaving to keep this appointment as arranged, I rang but there was no one there. I just had to risk keeping the appointment and go. I found the address with the security gate locked tight shut but when I knocked, someone answered. It turned out Mr 'Y' had been locked in. He dropped the key down from the window and I let myself in.

'Y', at 85 years old, is a piece of living history. As a youth in the 1930, he was a writer in the Modernist School, and found a refuge for his ideals with the Communist Party. For several decades he put his heart and soul into propagandising for the Party, becoming a high cultural official and denouncing other people as 'counter-revolutionaries'. He wrote children's stories to maintain a sense of self. Not until the Cultural Revolution when he himself was 'overthrown' did he have a real opportunity for sober reflection. He once said: 'In politics and culture I have drawn a circle, and in the end returned to the point where I started at 20 years old.' In the 1980s, he was one of the oldest members of Beijing's cultural youth groups. In 1989, he signed the petition demanding Wei Jingsheng's release, after which there was no news of him for a long time. I have not seen him for years but his mind is as agile as ever; the sad thing is that his wife, 'K', herself a poet and editor who was under a lifetime of political pressure has now developed a paranoid fear of being harmed, every day imagining someone is out to get her. This past decade or so, all of 'Y's energy has been spent on 'K' to the extent that he has been unable to get down to writing his memoirs. 'K' had gone out today with absolutely no news of when she would return, and had locked 'Y' into the flat. 'Y' could only smile sadly. 'A small detail.' What could I say? An age in miniature?

29 Dec 1999: In the morning, watch films at 'L's place on a video player (a necessity for every urban Chinese home) from the classic *Clockwork Orange* to the latest Hollywood productions, all, of course, pirate copies.

At noon, went out for a walk to the ruins of the Yuanming Gardens to reminisce and then decided to go with Mr 'T' to the flat his work-place has allocated him in Xi San Zu – the place I was sent with a work team during the Cultural Revolution … Should I have told 'T' that during the Cultural Revolution, only one minute's walk from his new home, 19 people were buried alive just because they were related to landlords?

From 'T's home, I got a 'black car' (unlicensed taxi) to Huangtu village. I could vaguely remember the way but when we got to the boundaries I was stunned: the whole village is a ruin. Between weeds and remaining snows were the broken and dilapidated walls. The road that had originally run north to south through the whole village has disappeared without trace …

The driver said all the land in the village has been sold to a real-estate developer. But because the villagers are not satisfied with their share of the 150 million RMB paid to the village government, clearing the land has been stopped and it remains wasteland to this day. However, an agreement has been reached where work will start on putting up buildings no later than March of next year, and concrete floors will finally bury all the memories.

I suddenly realised I was standing at a closing point in history. A village that had existed for who knows how many thousands of years and its ancient way of life was going to finish here. Among it was contained the three short years I had spent in this place.

30 Dec 1999: Got up at dawn and watched the television news of the four Falun Gong area organisers being sentenced. The details were that after Falun Gong was proclaimed an 'evil cult' [in July] they refused to renounce their beliefs and continued to organise meetings. The irony is that these four 'criminals' with their chests puffed out and heads held high, awesome in their fortitude and brimming with a martyr's air of dedication, strongly resembled the image of the archetypal 'Communist Party Hero' in official propaganda.

In the evening, the acclaimed number-one 'star' of literary circles, the poet and businessman 'L', had a dinner party ... Apart from the poets at the sumptuously laid table, there was also a certain stockbroker who is so powerful that when he moves the whole city shakes ... But China's stock market is currently in a severe slump. The small, ordinary investors have been stuck with devaluing shares so often that no matter what the government does to 'stimulate' the market, they still hold on to their money, stand back and observe. Recently, just before the Stock Market Management Law was issued, a big wave of publicity accompanied a large injection of funds on to the market, leading investors to believe the situation was robust and they quickly followed in. But who could have known that on the day the Management Law was announced, the funds would be withdrawn and the stock market would plummet? The majority of investors could not recuperate their original capital and my father was one of many who lost a lot of money.

31 Dec 1999: The last day of the 20th century; spent the morning at Yo Yo's mother's place, talking with her eldest son visiting from Lanzhou. He is a member of the post-1949 generation who lost out most on their modern education; all three of his siblings have either left the country or are working for Chinese companies with foreign connections; he is always grumbling in verse – China's contemporary oral literature:

> If you find your wages are down,
> The leaders are out in their Royal Crown.
> When your wages are down by a third,
> The leaders are seen in a big Blue Bird.
> When you're paid with a handful of beans,
> The leaders swan around in an Audi limousine.

(Royal Crown, Blue Bird and Audi are all imported luxury cars.)

We got a taxi to my brother's place in Fang Zhuang, then on to Zhao Gong Kou where we found a driver to take us to my father's home in Tianjin, not far from Beijing. Tianjin is a gloomy wasteland, completely lacking the extravagance and colour of Beijing's eating, drinking and entertainment. The streets are dreary and desolate with no sign of any festival atmosphere. The driver said it was because there are so many laid-off workers in Tianjin – originally a centre for state-owned enterprises. With so many people on only 200 RMB a month and barely able to feed themselves, what is there to celebrate? He said: 'In the old days, the working classes were the first in line, but now the state has just kicked them out. They sell their whole life and in the end they're just sacrificial goods. What a farce!'

My younger brother, the businessman who works himself into the ground, has managed to find the time to come with us. We, my father and my brother's girlfriend went as a family to a restaurant we had booked for a new year's meal. All the restaurant rooms between 400 and 800 RMB had already been taken – even though we were in Tianjin. The two bottles of wine I had brought all the way from Europe added a touch of colour to the meal and in our room was a television so we could eat and watch the live broadcast of the new year celebrations at the same time. This year, for the first time, Beijing Central Television was broadcasting reports sent by specially posted journalists in Sydney, Paris, London and New York, cutting them into their own 24-hour non-stop new year programming.

But China's official celebration programme was still full of the same old government propaganda: Jiang Zemin's congratulatory speech; the Party and state leaders lining up in public; China's Millennium Temple (modelled on the old imperial Temple of Heaven and Temple of Earth); China's Millennium Bell (extending the millennia-old imperial tradition of the 'Bell Casting' ceremony), all in a cold snap more than ten degrees below zero, with thousands of people (including children) singing and dancing in colourful but thin costumes. The recent 'return' of Macao was, of course, a main theme. The repeated appearance of the characters for 'Taiwan' made clear the next objective of 'Unification of the Motherland'. The ostentatious opulence, the celebration of extravagance, the care and attention paid to highlighting 'Times of Peace and Prosperity' was, in comparison with the plight of laid-off workers in

Tianjin, both ironic and very distant.

After the meal we went back to our father's home to spend the last few minutes of the 20th century talking about our family's experiences over the last decades: my father was born into the household of a wealthy Han merchant and Manchu aristocracy. After graduating from the Catholic Furen University before he was 20, he cut himself off from his 'exploiting family' and joined the communist revolution. His whole life since then has been spent watching all his dreams from his early years being shattered one by one. His wisdom lay in realising when to withdraw during the insanity of that age: from being a foreign diplomat to working in a university; from being an 'old revolutionary' professor to being the 'backward element' who fell asleep in public meetings. I suggest to him: 'The greatest achievement in your life has been that you achieved nothing.' At least this has offered him some inner peace in the later years of his life. But the reality is still turbulent: the old cadres' pension cannot keep up with sky-rocketing prices and were it not for the support from my brother and sister my father would still be relying on his own efforts. He has already spent two years of 'study fees' on the stock exchange and hopes this year he can start making a profit (even though the news about Lan Tian is enough to make you cry). 'But don't you think from the time you turned your back on your family until now has been a wasted journey?' I asked. My father smiled sadly at the only answer he could give: 'I can only think of the people who have had it worse than me.'

As the new year bells rang, my feelings were (at least as far as the people of China can say) at last, we have made it through the 20th century!

In one more second, completely new numbers must be used to write this epoch. But will the century truly be new? ❑

Yang Lian is a Chinese poet living in London
Translated by Ben Carrdus